Awakening the Great White North

A Journey to Reclaim Canada's Destiny

Written by:
Alan E Shields

INDEX

Prologue

In the quaint Laurentian village of Saint Sauveur, Quebec, nestled among the rolling hills and whispering pines, Alan Shields gazed at the world through a lens of innovation. As a seasoned inventor, he was no stranger to the thrill of seeing his ideas take shape, but nothing had prepared him for the magnum opus that would become the GlobeTrotter Ecosystem.

As a young boy, Alan was inspired by tales of great inventors and visionaries, who not only changed the world but also envisioned its future. With a mind that constantly whirred and churned, dissecting every machine, every system, every aspect of life, he grew into a man capable of reimagining the very fabric of society.

The Canada he knew was transforming, and as the winds of change blew colder and more turbulent, Alan felt an increasing responsibility to harness those gusts and direct them towards a future of hope, prosperity, and true democracy. Yet, it wasn't just the nation's politics that drove him—it was personal. It was the love for his family, the memories shared with loved ones, the scent of home, and the bonds that ran deeper than the Saint Lawrence River.

This tale, though rooted in realistic fiction, stems from the very essence of Alan's life—a life that's very real. While his past is a testament to his tenacity and creativity, his envisioned future, powered by the GlobeTrotter Ecosystem, is a beacon of hope. A hope that maybe, just maybe, if one man can dream it, a nation can live it.

So, as you embark on this journey through the pages of 'Awakening the Great White North', remember that while some events and characters may be a product of the author's imagination, the spirit of change, of resistance, and of reclamation, is as real as the northern lights that paint the Canadian skies.

Welcome to a vision of Canada's possible future—one man's dream for his beloved homeland. Welcome to Alan Shields' legacy.

5

Chapter 1

A Distant Home

Sunlight streaked through the dusty windows of the workshop in Piedmont, Qc, casting long shadows over worktables laden with tools, materials, and the beginnings of various creations. The gentle hum of machinery harmonized with the rhythmic tapping of hammers, producing a calming, methodical melody. In the center, Alan, with a pair of safety goggles resting atop his head, concentrated on crafting a chandelier. His hands, marked by time and labor, moved with precision as they connected wrought iron segments, creating a skeletal structure. As he worked, he was lost in thought, every move a testament to years of dedication and craftsmanship.

Beside him, Tony, his younger brother, was deeply engrossed in refining details on a large wooden beam, which would soon become a part of an impressive fireplace mantel. Their bond was palpable, evident in their silent communication, a glance or a subtle gesture enough to convey meaning. The nephews, younger and more energetic, working on their own projects, assisting and learning. Their laughter and occasional playful banter contrasted the serious concentration of their elders, adding a youthful vibrancy to the otherwise tranquil environment.

Across the workshop was Alan's office, a fascinating juxtaposition of the old and the new. The door, repurposed from a barn, led into a haven for an inventor's mind. Walls, adorned with sketches, flowed like a river of creativity, each drawing more intricate than the last. Amidst the organized chaos of papers, pencils, and rulers, half-finished prototypes sat proudly, waiting for their moment of completion. From energy storage devices to miniature environmental energy-producing machines, they hinted at the brilliance and depth of Alan's innovative spirit. One could sense that the room was a manifestation of a constantly churning mind, always on the cusp of the next great idea.

The chandelier, now taking shape under the workshop's ambient lighting, was momentarily forgotten as Alan's attention gravitated towards a project closer to his heart. On one of the worktables lay a curious contraption, a mesh of metals and wires, its purpose not immediately apparent to the untrained eye. With furrowed brows, Alan delved deep into a notebook filled with calculations, each page representing hours of thought, trial, and reiteration. The margins were filled with quick notes, sketches, and formulas. Every so often, he'd pause, adjust a component on the device, scribble down an observation, and then lose himself in contemplation once more. This energy storage device was his latest venture, a potential solution to the increasing demands of a rapidly modernizing world.

In the background, a vintage radio, a relic from the past amidst the cutting-edge tools, played softly, almost as if not to disturb the master at work. Its nostalgic tunes would occasionally be interrupted by the voice of a news anchor, conveying snippets of daily happenings. "In Ottawa today, Prime Minister Justin Trudeau addressed the nation," the radio broadcasted, its tone neutral, but the underlying message evident to any discerning listener. The political climate in Canada was becoming increasingly tumultuous, with policies and decisions often reflecting a shift away from traditional Canadian values. Alan, though engrossed in his work, couldn't help but occasionally pause and absorb the words, each news segment fueling a growing concern.

Subsequent news segments touched on varied subjects: economic forecasts, international relations, but most importantly, glimpses into the government's vision for Canada's future. The underlying narrative was clear. There were elements pushing for a change, transformations that didn't always sit well with the broader public. While Alan's primary focus remained on his inventions, these snippets from the outside world were constant reminders of the shifting sands of the Canadian political landscape.

From the vintage radio's worn-out speakers, a familiar voice emerged, commanding in tone yet polished in its delivery. It was an exclusive interview with Prime Minister Justin Trudeau. Alan's hand, which had been meticulously tweaking his device, stilled momentarily. He leaned back, the gears in his mind momentarily shifting away from engineering designs to the content of the interview. Trudeau was articulating his vision for Canada—a nation that would lead by example, a beacon for others to emulate. As the Prime Minister continued, Alan's face grew taut, each word chiseling into his features a mix of incredulity and concern. This wasn't the Canada he had grown up in nor the one he had hoped future generations would inherit.

As Trudeau's voice echoed with promises of a brighter tomorrow, Alan's mind wandered to the not-so-distant past. Memories bubbled up uninvited images of the Covid crisis, streets filled with a restless energy, the deafening honks of the trucker convoy, the resonance of their protests symbolizing the voices of thousands. These weren't just news segments; they had become part of the nation's lived reality. Alan recalled heated debates with friends, articles highlighting frozen bank accounts, and rumors of governmental bullying tactics. A heavy sigh escaped him. The vision Trudeau painted seemed increasingly detached from the ground realities many Canadians were experiencing.

Each memory seemed to add weight to Alan's shoulders. The raw emotions of the people, their pleas for transparency, and the alleged government's iron-fisted approach to dissent—it all played like a montage in his mind. The radio continued its broadcast, Trudeau's polished rhetoric juxtaposed starkly against Alan's visceral memories. The incongruity of it all was jarring. For Alan, this moment was a catalyst, a sudden coalescence of thoughts and emotions. He was already contemplating steps towards greater self-reliance through his inventions, but the mounting political concerns indicated that perhaps the time for broader action was drawing near.

Sitting in his workshop, amidst the blueprints of his countless inventions, Alan was suddenly gripped by an overwhelming realization. Canada, his beloved homeland, was not just faltering—it needed a fundamental rebuilding, a rebirth. The mounting political corruption, the distance between the governing elites and the everyday Canadian, and the eroding freedoms had all become too palpable to ignore. His eyes landed on a set of papers, dust-covered but still pristine—the preliminary designs for the GlobeTrotter Ecosystem. An ambitious project he had shelved years ago, considering it too vast and ahead of its time. But now, Alan saw it with newfound clarity. The GlobeTrotter Ecosystem wasn't just an innovative project; it could be the very cornerstone of Canada's resurrection. It was time to take this dormant dream off the backburner, breathe life into it, and offer Canada not just hope but a tangible path to redemption.

The sun set low over Saint Sauveur, its orange and pink hues painting a vivid backdrop against the silhouetted Laurentians. In a small, intimate cafe, Alan sat across from Chantal, the warmth from the steaming cups of herbal tea barely registering. "I've made a decision, Sweety," Alan began, locking eyes with her. Chantal's gaze was unwavering, her intuitive nature sensing the gravity of what he was about to say. "I'm thinking of leaving Canada... for Mexico." The weight of his declaration hung in the air, juxtaposed against the ambient laughter and chatter of the cafe. Chantal's eyes searched his, seeking understanding, seeking reasons. "Mexico? Why so far?" she asked, her voice barely above a whisper. The tremble in her voice betrayed her attempt at composure. "I need a change, a break from all this. The political climate, the disillusionment. Mexico might be that fresh start, that respite, and a quiet place for me to work on my new system" he explained, his conviction evident.

Chantal reached across the table, her fingers lightly brushing against his. "Isn't this just running away, Alan? Escaping the challenges rather than facing them?" she probed gently. He sighed, running a hand through his hair. "I've asked myself that a million times. But is it really running away, or is it seeking clarity? Sometimes, to understand a situation, to really see it, you need to step out of it. Gain perspective." His gaze drifted momentarily, landing on a family laughing together at a nearby table. "Canada's my home, always will be. But the home I once knew has changed, and I'm not sure if I can just stand by and watch."

The herbal tea grew cold, but the conversation between them remained fervent. As Chantal listened, she began to grasp the depths of Alan's internal struggle. The duality of his feelings was palpable. On one hand, the inventor, the problem-solver in him, nagged him for retreating from a challenge. Yet, the man who had seen his homeland shift into an unfamiliar terrain felt a profound need to recalibrate, to rediscover purpose in a place free from the shadows of his memories and disappointments. Mexico, with its rich culture, vibrant landscapes, and promise of a fresh perspective, beckoned him. It offered an opportunity to breathe, reflect, and perhaps find a way to reconcile with the changes happening in the land he loved.

Chapter 2

Unsettling News

Mexico greeted Alan with an embrace of warmth, tropic smells, and vibrant colors. Each morning, as the sun rose above the horizon, casting brilliant hues of gold and crimson across the sky, he would find himself walking along the sandy beaches. The coastline stretched endlessly, with azure waters kissing the shores, leaving behind a trail of white frothy remnants. Beautiful women, their skin sun-kissed, draped in vibrant bikinis, played beach volleyball or lounged under oversized straw hats. Alan often found solace in these walks, the rhythmic cadence of waves serenading his thoughts. On weekends, the bustling markets came alive, with vendors calling out their offers, and the tantalizing aroma of freshly prepared Mexican delicacies wafting through the air. Everywhere he looked, there was a burst of color – from handcrafted pottery, intricate textiles, to lush tropical fruits. The scent of the tropics - a mix of the salty sea, sweet fruits, and the smoky allure of grilled meats - pervaded the air.

As the sun bid adieu, painting the town with shadows and soft light, Alan's evenings took a different turn. The rhythmic sound of waves was replaced by the shuffling of poker cards and light-hearted banter. Ron, a stout man with a graying beard and an affinity for colorful Hawaiian shirts, owned the local beach bar and was always the one to deal the cards. Valentin, a French native with deep-set eyes and a sharp wit, had stories that spanned from local legends to the latest town gossip. Dave and Curtis, two ex-pats like Alan, had also found solace in the sandy beaches of Mexico. Dave, a former Wall Street banker, had tales of high-stakes trading, while Curtis, a retired marine biologist, spoke of the mysteries of the deep. These poker nights were not just about the game; they were sessions filled with camaraderie, laughter, and moments of introspection.

Within this close-knit circle, Alan found a semblance of home. Each had their reasons for being in Mexico, their tales of escapism or pursuit. Their shared evenings under the canopy of stars, with the distant sound of the ocean as a constant companion, created a bond. Even in a foreign land, amidst the vibrancy and chaos, Alan carved out a space that felt familiar. His social circle, though diverse in backgrounds and stories, provided a haven where he could be himself, reflecting on the past while embracing the vibrancy of the present.

Each day, as dawn broke, Alan would set out on his walks, a ritual he adhered to religiously. The initial walks were an escape, a way to leave behind the chaos of his thoughts, but over time, they morphed into moments of solitude and clarity. The cobbled streets of Playa del Carmen, with their rich history and old-world charm, often acted as a muse, inspiring him to think, reflect, and dream. Local kids would often run past him, their laughter echoing through the narrow alleyways. Elderly women, with their weathered faces and tales of a time gone by, would often sit outside, weaving or selling fresh produce. Alan's steps would often synchronize with the rhythm of life around him — sometimes hurried, as he'd dodge a vendor or two, and sometimes leisurely, allowing him to absorb the beauty around. These walks, besides giving him fresh air and exercise, became a source of inspiration for his writing.

Alan's condo was an eclectic mix of traditional Mexican architecture and personal touches. At the center of his living room lay a mahogany desk, strewn with manuscripts, scribbles, drafts, his computer, and a vintage typewriter as a decoration. Some papers bore the beginnings of a new novel; others were filled with poetic verses inspired by his surroundings, but most importantly were his white paper for the GlobeTrotter Ecosystem. He worked every day on this for the last year and it was pretty much completed. The walls of his home office were lined with bookshelves, holding a collection that ranged from classic literature to modern thrillers. A beautiful tropical plant occupied a corner, next to a state-of-the-art home theater system. Alan's evenings often oscillated between watching old western classics, where he'd lose himself in tales of love and valor, and binge-watching the latest TV shows, a guilty pleasure that he often indulged in. This space was a testament to his diverse interests, a blend of the old and the new, mirroring his evolving self.

However, even in this newfound tranquility, Alan's entrepreneurial spirit couldn't be stifled. One day when he went to Tulum, he noticed the inefficiency of public transportation and the growing number of tourists struggling with mobility. An idea began to form: a small bus line tailored to the needs of tourists and locals alike. This wasn't just a business venture for Alan; it was a puzzle, a challenge to innovate and provide a solution that would blend seamlessly into the town's fabric. Preliminary plans were sketched out, and soon meetings with local authorities and potential investors were scheduled. This endeavor, like many of his past projects, was a testament to Alan's insatiable drive to create and contribute. He was not just a visitor in Mexico; he intended to leave an imprint, combining his expertise with his love for his adopted home.

It was a typical Friday night at Alan's condo. The warm Mexican air carried the distant sounds of a mariachi band, mingling with the clinking of poker chips and raucous laughter. The table was littered with an assortment of colorful cards, drinks, and poker chips, the glow from the overhead lamp casting dancing shadows on the gathered faces. But the jovial atmosphere was abruptly shattered when Dave's phone, lying next to his stack of chips, emitted a sharp ring, signaling a news alert. The laughter ceased as Dave picked up his phone, his face turning grave as he read the headlines. As the words spilled from Dave's lips, the atmosphere in the room grew tense. Alan's face, which moments ago had been animated with jest and cheer, transformed into a mask of deep concern and simmering anger. Each word from the alert acted like a dagger, reminding him of the homeland he had left behind, yet whose ties still tugged at his heartstrings.

Ron, noticing Alan's intense reaction, attempted to lighten the mood with a playful jest. However, the effort fell flat, and a heavy silence enveloped the group. Valentin, always the inquisitive one, couldn't resist probing further. "I never realized just how deeply Canada resonates with you, Alan," he commented. This simple observation opened a floodgate of memories and feelings. With a deep sigh, Alan began recounting tales of his childhood, the crisp Canadian winters, the warmth of community festivals, and the pride of belonging to a nation known for its values and harmony. His narratives painted a vivid picture of a country rich in traditions, diversity, and unity.

As the night deepened, so did the conversation. Curtis, a history enthusiast, chimed in with his knowledge of Canada's political past, while Dave shared stories from his brief visit to Vancouver. The conversation shifted from personal anecdotes to heated debates about global politics. Alan found himself at the center, passionately defending his homeland's virtues while acknowledging its flaws. The poker chips and cards lay forgotten as the men, fueled by tequila and a genuine thirst for knowledge, delved into a profound discussion about Canada's identity, challenges, and the hope for a better future. What started as a casual poker night turned into a testament of Alan's undying connection to Canada, and his friends got a glimpse into the depth of his attachment and the concerns that weighed heavily on his heart.

Chapter 3

Echoes of the Past

The shimmering sands and balmy breezes of Mexico were a stark contrast to the wintry wonderland that Quebec transformed into each year. Alan would often close his eyes, allowing his senses to transport him back to those crisp, icy mornings. He'd envision stepping out of his home, a cloud of breath preceding him, as the delicate crunch of fresh snow underfoot filled his ears. Streets, once familiar in their everyday drabness, turned magical overnight, the snow acting as a canvas, reflecting the soft glow of streetlights and the twinkle of early Christmas decorations. Each home seemed to emanate warmth, with tendrils of smoke rising from chimneys, carrying with them the nostalgic scent of burning wood. The occasional carolers, bundled up in scarves and hats, added a melodic backdrop to this picturesque setting. Every sound, muffled and serene, brought forth a tranquility that Alan hadn't realized he missed so dearly.

Chantal had always been a child at heart when it came to snow. Alan chuckled to himself as he remembered a particular day. The two of them, fresh from an indoor date involving hot cocoa and an old movie, had spontaneously decided to venture out into the snowstorm. Before Alan knew what was happening, a snowball hit him squarely in the chest. He looked up to see Chantal, her nose reddened from the cold, trying her best to suppress a mischievous grin. That evening, the yard in Prévost became their playground. The world around them disappeared as they dodged, ducked, and retaliated in what became an epic snowball showdown. It wasn't just the playful fights that he reminisced about; it was the moments of stillness between. When hands numbed from the cold, they would embrace. Alan remembered how Chantal's touch, always warm, felt like a beacon in the icy chill. Those instances, when the world faded and only the two of them existed, were when he felt most connected to her.

Chantal had this innate ability to care deeply, and that winter was no exception. As the days grew colder, her caring nature blossomed. She'd insist on him wearing an extra layer, or ensuring he had his gloves before they stepped out. There were times she'd surprise him with a home-cooked meal, rich and hearty, perfect for the weather. And on days when the snowfall was particularly heavy, she'd call him, her voice laced with concern, asking if he'd made it home safely. It was these little things, these daily affirmations of love and care, that made Alan realize how deeply he was ensnared in her web of affection. Every snowflake, every gust of cold wind, became a testament to their growing bond.

The New Year's Eve parties at Lise's home weren't just simple gatherings; they were a culmination of love, laughter, and family bonding. The spacious living room would be adorned with glimmering decorations, the golden and silver hues reflecting the gleaming hope of a new year. A cuckoo clock would tick away on the wall, a reminder of the fleeting moments and the promise of new beginnings. As the evening sun dipped and night began its ascent, one could hear the gentle hum of chatter, the clinking of glasses, and the boisterous laughter echoing through the halls. Alan fondly remembered how his mother Lise, ever the gracious host, would have her home buzzing with activity.

Amongst the laughter and chatter, memories from New Year's Eve parties at Alan's mother's home flood back, providing warmth and nostalgia. It's these gatherings where bonds strengthened, stories were shared, and everyone came together as one unit. Lise, Alan's aging mother, remains the pillar of the family, her tales and advice providing a beacon for many. Monica, Alan's sister, and her husband JP, along with their curious son Gabriel, always lit up the room. Then there's Tony, Alan's vivacious younger brother, with his wife Dina, and their bustling brood of five: Ariel, Benjamin, Saphire, Tao-Lin, and Christiam, each with a unique spark of their own. Lorraine, the ever-cheerful aunt, never missed an opportunity to spread joy. David, Alan's eldest, stood proudly with Sabrina, his partner, watching over their two precious daughters, Amélia and Liana, their laughter echoing the hopes of a bright future. Amid the bustle of such gatherings, there was always a special corner for Chantal, always radiant in her laughter, their son Nathaniel, whose antics often became the highlight of the evening, and his lovely girlfriend Irena, whose charm and warmth quickly endeared her to the family. Completing the tapestry is Lise's husband's extended family - Marc, with his calm demeanor and wife Céline, alongside the effervescent Christine, always bringing fresh perspectives to their conversations. Each family member, with their distinct characteristics and essence, painted a vivid picture of love, unity, and shared history.

Amidst this whirlwind of personalities and the cacophony of family joy, the bond between Alan and his mother Lise stood out. It wasn't just in the shared smiles, the knowing glances, or the whispered secrets. It was deeper, almost palpable. Alan, even amidst the festivities, would often catch himself observing Lise. He would watch as she, with grace and poise, would navigate through the crowd, her laughter echoing, her hands touching, comforting, and guiding. But there were moments, fleeting yet heavy, when he would notice the tiredness in her eyes, the slight slump of her shoulders, the sigh escaping her lips. The reality of her advancing age weighed heavily on him. Each wrinkle, each gray strand was a stark reminder of the impermanence of life. It made him treasure these moments even more, etching them deep into his memory, to be revisited during lonely nights in Mexico.

The Playa del Carmen beach club, with its pristine white sands and azure waters, was where Alan often sought solace. Today, the club was abuzz with tourists soaking in the sun and families playing by the shore. Alan, however, was an island amidst the crowd, lost in thought. His favorite spot was a hammock strung between two palm trees. Lying there, with the Caribbean sun warming his face, Alan tried to silence the internal debate raging inside him. He had come to Mexico to escape, to find a semblance of peace away from the tumultuous events of his homeland. And he had found it — the simplicity of life here, the lack of political entanglements, and the sheer beauty of the place had healed him in ways he hadn't imagined. But every time he closed his eyes, images of the colored trees in the Fall time, his family's laughter, time with Chantal, his son Nathaniel and his soon-to-be wife Irena, and the comforting smell of his mother's cooking beckoned him. The two worlds were poles apart, and the decision to choose between them weighed heavily on his heart.

As the sun began its descent, painting the sky with hues of orange and pink, Alan's phone buzzed. It was Chantal. He took a deep breath before answering. Her voice, a familiar and comforting tune, washed over him. "Alan... How are you?" she began tentatively, knowing well that this wasn't just a casual check-in. Their conversation treaded softly around the real issues, with each sentence layered with years of shared memories, unsaid words, and buried feelings. Alan spoke of his life in Mexico, the friends he had made, and the small ventures he was a part of. Chantal spoke of Quebec, the changes since he left, and how much he was missed. There was a pause, filled with static and heavy breathing. Then, with a voice that wavered just slightly, Chantal whispered, "We need you here Alan. You could do more good here than in Mexico" That was the crux of their conversation — the unspoken plea, the silent hope.

When Alan finally hung up, the decision had been made. The evening sky was now a deep shade of purple, with stars beginning to twinkle in the distance. The soothing sound of waves crashing onto the shore filled the void of silence. The comfort and allure of Mexico had been a balm to his wounded spirit. But the pull of his homeland, the memories of snow-covered streets, and most importantly, the love and bonds of his family, were impossible to ignore. With newfound resolve, Alan decided — it was time to return. The GlobeTrotter Ecosystem was ready and time to put it into motion. The journey ahead wouldn't be easy, but the decision, made amidst the backdrop of a Playa del Carmen sunset, felt right.

Alan did everything that needed to be done in his condo for his departure, making sure it would be ready and waiting when he comes back. He said his goodbyes to his friends and Ron offered to bring him to the Cancun airport, which Alan happily accepted. The day arrived and Ron was there waiting. Alan brought down his suitcase and backpack and off they went to the airport. Alan looking at everything on the way taking in all the beauty.

Chapter 4

The Return

The plane descended, giving Alan a panoramic view of Montreal. From his window seat, he could see the city's sprawl, the patches of vibrant fall colors juxtaposed with the gray and brown hues of the urban expanse. There was an irony in landing at Montreal's Trudeau airport, given his turbulent relationship with the policies and vision of the very namesake of this place. He had left the sun-kissed shores of Mexico, a paradise where every day felt like an endless summer. Now, stepping off the plane, Alan was immediately greeted by the nippy chill of a Quebec Fall. The airport was abuzz with people - families reuniting, travelers chatting, the intercom announcing the next departures. Yet for Alan, it was like stepping into a still frame from his past. The signs in French, the familiar timbre of Quebecois accents, and even the distinct cold were all reminders of what he had left behind.

As he walked through the terminal, every step brought a flood of emotions and memories. The overhead lights seemed brighter, the sounds more pronounced, and every corner seemed to stir some distant recollection. Alan felt a tightness in his chest – a mix of dread and excitement. Was he ready to start over again? The vibrant images of Mexico - its beaches, its people, its music – seemed worlds away, yet they had been his reality just a few hours ago. Now, the dimmed lighting of the airport, the hurried travelers, and the muted colors of a North American fall were pushing those sunny memories into the background. He took a deep breath, trying to anchor himself amidst the sensory overload.

Exiting the terminal, Alan scanned the faces of those waiting. His eyes landed on the familiar figure of his brother, Tony. Their eyes met, and in an instant, years of brotherhood, memories, and shared secrets passed between them. Tony's characteristic grin spread across his face, a silent acknowledgment of their bond. While time had added a few gray strands to Tony's hair and a hint of weariness around his eyes, his jovial spirit remained unchanged. They embraced, a powerful hug that communicated more than words ever could. Alan could feel Tony's silent reassurances and the depth of their bond. In that single moment, surrounded by the hustle and bustle of the airport, the two brothers found solace in their reunion. Alan was home, and with Tony by his side, he felt ready to face the next chapter.

Arriving in Saint Sauveur, it has always been a gem nestled amidst the verdant Quebec landscape. A town where nature met human craftsmanship to create a harmonious balance. Its streets, lined with trees in radiant hues, from the evergreens to the fiery shades of autumn leaves, contrasted and complemented the rustic charm of its structures. The historic buildings, some with walls weathered by time and tales, showcased intricate designs, a testament to the rich history and the artistic flair of the locals. Among these, the quaint cafes were particularly delightful. The inviting aroma of fresh pastries and coffee served as a beacon for both locals and visitors, offering a warm embrace and a momentary escape from the world outside.

As Tony steered his vehicle into the town's center, every landmark he passed seemed to whisper stories of the days gone by. There was the old library, where he'd spent countless hours parked in front of as a teenager on his motorcycle. A left turn took him past the park where he'd watched people play soccer on sunny afternoons. Each street, every corner evoked a memory – some vividly clear, others faded but fond. The playground with the rusty swings, the bakery with the best croissants, the bridge overlooking the tranquil river where he had shared many silent moments with Chantal – it felt like a nostalgic journey through time.

The deeper Alan drove into Saint Sauveur, the more overwhelming his emotions became. It was a blend of warmth from the familiarity and a sting from the memories of the times that had led him to leave. Every honk, every distant chatter, the familiar tune from the church's bell, even the cool breeze that brushed against his face seemed imbued with a sense of homecoming. But with that also came the realization of how much he had missed, how many moments he had lost, and the weight of the choices he had made. Amidst these reflections, the sight of a particular house with blue shutters made his heart race – he was close to his mother's home.

As Alan stepped onto the familiar wooden porch of his mom's home, a wave of nostalgia enveloped him. The creaking sound of the wooden door, the lingering aroma of freshly baked bread, and the walls that held memories of years gone by beckoned him in. Before he could knock, the door gently swung open, revealing the comforting figure of Lise. Her blond hair shimmered under the soft indoor light, and her age-wrinkled face bore the lines of time, wisdom, and a boundless love for her son. They didn't need words; their eyes spoke volumes. With tears threatening to spill, she pulled him into a warm embrace. That night, Alan slept in the spare bedroom, surrounded by remnants of his past. The old room, with its familiar scent and warmth, became his sanctuary in the days to come as he attempted to rebuild his life piece by piece.

The following day was filled with the sort of chaos only a family reunion could bring. The air resonated with laughter, joy, and a cacophony of voices that Alan had missed dearly. Tony, with his signature boisterous laugh, was the first to greet him, recounting tales of their childhood mischief. Monica, with her ever-patient demeanor, playfully teased the two brothers for acting like they were still teenagers. Their spouses seamlessly wove themselves into the fabric of the gathering, each adding their unique flavor to the tapestry of memories being created. As the adult kids moved about, their innocent giggles and playful shrieks punctuating the air, Alan couldn't help but marvel at the passage of time. From Ariel's attempts to show off his soccer skills to Tao-Lin's enthusiastic storytelling, each one added a touch of wonder to the day.

The evening saw the entire family huddled around the dinner table; a sumptuous feast spread out before them. As dishes were passed around and glasses clinked in celebration, light-hearted banter took center stage. Alan found himself the target of many a joke, mostly revolving around his extended 'vacation' in Mexico. Yet, beneath the laughter and teasing, a subtle current of concern and understanding flowed. It was evident that while they celebrated his return, there was an underlying appreciation for the journey he had undertaken, both physically and emotionally. It was in these moments, amidst the stories, laughter, and familial warmth, that Alan truly realized what he had left behind and what he had now reclaimed.

Alan had played the moment of reunion in his head a thousand times, but nothing could have prepared him for the actual encounter with Chantal. The restaurant they chose was intimate, with dim lighting and a soft murmur of conversation that provided a suitable backdrop for their own conversation. As he stepped inside, he caught sight of Chantal seated at a corner table, engrossed in a menu. As their eyes met, a rush of emotions hit Alan, leaving him momentarily breathless. Her beauty was timeless, but it was her eyes, as deep and mysterious as ever, that captivated him once more. Nathaniel, now a young man with a strong resemblance to Alan, was seated next to her. Irena, with her radiant smile, sat on Nathaniel's other side. All three greeted Alan warmly, making the ambiance lighter and less tense.

The conversation flowed more easily than Alan anticipated. They spoke about everything and nothing - recent movies, Nathaniel's business plans, Irena's art exhibitions. But beneath the surface of those casual topics was a palpable tension, an unspoken acknowledgment of the depth of their shared history. There were moments when Alan and Chantal's eyes would lock, and both would be lost in memories of days gone by. The weight of their past was always lurking, casting shadows on the present. Chantal seemed hopeful yet cautious, her optimism evident in her gentle probing about Alan's plans and his life in Mexico. Alan talked about his time in Mexico, how wonderful it was. That he had worked on his new system to help Canada renew its greatness and that he planned on trying to implement it. Yet, there was a defensive wall around her, hinting at past hurts and betrayals.

As the evening wore on, Alan felt an overwhelming mix of guilt for leaving and a renewed longing for the life and love he had left behind. Every so often, he would catch a guarded look in Chantal's eyes, reminding him of the pain his departure had caused. However, interspersed with these moments were flashes of the love and camaraderie they once shared. It was clear that their bond, though strained, had not been severed. Both were treading cautiously, neither willing to expose their vulnerable hearts fully. But the spark between them was undeniable. As they said their goodbyes, with promises to meet again tomorrow night for dinner at Chantal's, Alan felt a glimmer of hope that perhaps, just perhaps, they could find their way back to each other.

Chapter 5

Gathering Storm

The atmosphere inside Alan's mother's living room was heavy. On the television, journalists with serious expressions delivered the latest updates on Canada's political scene. Images of large-scale protests, impassioned speeches from both politicians and citizens, and the occasional chaos of a rally gone wrong flashed across the screen. Alan leaned forward, every muscle in his body taut as he absorbed the information. The unease he had felt earlier was now deepening into a genuine worry. Each news clip served as evidence that the country he loved was on the brink of something significant and potentially catastrophic. The underlying tensions he had sensed from afar were not just figments of his imagination. They were real, tangible, and threatening to pull apart the very fabric of Canadian society.

Alan sat next to his mother, taking a moment to choose the right words, knowing he had to simplify the enormity of his vision. "Mom," he began, his voice soft but charged with conviction, "imagine a Canada where everyone, regardless of their background or circumstances, has a basic income. Where every person's voice truly counts and where the unnecessary complexities of banks and taxes are a thing of the past. The GlobeTrotter Ecosystem is designed to eliminate the dark shadows of corruption, to ensure businesses give back to society, and to foster an environment where creativity and innovation thrive. It's not just about financial change, but about rebuilding Canada with transparency, fairness, and a renewed sense of community at its core."

Lise looked deeply into Alan's eyes, her expression a blend of pride and maternal understanding. "Oh, Alan," she sighed, her voice warm and tinged with nostalgia, "ever since you were a little boy, you've had that spark in you—the spark of a dreamer. You've never been one to shy away from the big problems, always wanting to make the world a better place. Your father and I used to say you'd move mountains one day. This... this GlobeTrotter Ecosystem of yours, it's just another mountain you're setting out to move, isn't it?" She smiled gently, reaching out to touch his face. "Just promise me you'll be careful, my dreamer."

That night at Chantal's home, the dining area was warmly lit, creating a cozy ambiance. The familiar scents from her kitchen reminded Alan of earlier times. As the table was meticulously set, the delicious aroma of a home-cooked meal filled the room, drawing everyone closer. Alan took a seat, with Chantal on one side and the young couple, Nathaniel and Irena, on the other. There was a brief moment of calm, punctuated only by the sound of cutlery being adjusted and water being poured. However, the quiet didn't last long. The country's escalating political situation was the elephant in the room, and Nathaniel, ever passionate, was the first to address it. He laid out his apprehensions about what the future held for him, expressing his dismay over the dwindling job prospects and the overall unstable socio-political atmosphere. Irena, her grip tightening around Nathaniel's hand, spoke up about her own circles, detailing the struggles and fears engulfing the arts community she belonged to.

As the night deepened, the conversation grew more intense. Chantal, always the voice of reason, tried to bring in a balanced perspective, pointing out areas where there might be hope or potential for change. But even she couldn't hide her own apprehensions, especially when it came to the safety and security of her family. Alan, his protective instincts flaring, promised that he would be there for them, come what may. The gravity of the situation was not lost on any of them. It was clear that Canada was at a crossroads, and the choices made in the coming months would determine its trajectory for decades or even generations. The family dinner, which began with lighthearted banter, ended with a renewed sense of purpose and a commitment to face the gathering storm together.

As the weight of their individual concerns pressed down on the room, Alan felt the moment was ripe to introduce his vision for the GlobeTrotter Ecosystem. He leaned forward, drawing everyone's attention. "You know," he began, capturing their collective gaze, "I've been working on something for a while now. Something I believe can redefine the landscape of this country." Chantal exchanged glances with Nathaniel and Irena, curiosity evident in their eyes. "It's called the GlobeTrotter Ecosystem," Alan continued, pausing briefly to gauge their reactions. "Imagine a world free from the corruption, abuse of power, and disparity we see today. Where every individual's voice truly counts. A revamped economic system that guarantees a basic income and job for everyone, eliminating poverty and reducing the power of the elites." Nathaniel leaned in, intrigued. "It's based on a new global currency, transparently controlled by everyone. The ecosystem automates fairness, transparency, and equality, irrespective of any external influences." Irena's eyes lit up, "So, a new beginning for Canada?" Alan nodded, "Exactly. A chance for Canada to be a beacon of hope in a world that's increasingly darkening. It's been on the backburner for a while, but I believe now is the time for its fruition." Chantal sighed, "Alan, this could change everything." The room, which had been filled with apprehension just moments ago, now hummed with a new energy, a flicker of hope.

Alan had always been tech-savvy, a trait that saw him actively participate in various online forums even before he moved to Mexico. Now, back in Canada and seeking to gain a deeper understanding of the ongoing political turmoil, he once again delved into the digital world. Logging in felt like entering a familiar room after a long absence. The screen lit up with notifications, messages from old threads, and updates from communities he was once an integral part of. These forums, ranging from political discussions to technological innovations, had always been his window to the world, a place where he could gauge the pulse of people from different walks of life.

As he skimmed through various discussions, Alan was impressed by the depth of conversations and the wealth of knowledge shared by members. It was a stark contrast to the snippets and headlines he'd been exposed to on mainstream media. With a few clicks, he joined some of the more heated debates, rekindling connections with individuals he recognized and getting acquainted with newer members. The sense of community was palpable, even in the vast expanse of cyberspace. Here, ideas flowed freely, beyond the clutches of geographical boundaries or physical identities.

A unique feature of these forums was the blend of anonymity and transparency. While many members, valuing their privacy or wary of potential backlash, chose to use pseudonyms, others boldly introduced themselves with their real names. This mixture created a dynamic environment where a person's arguments were valued based on their merit rather than their identity. Alan found this refreshing. He was particularly drawn to a chat thread where individuals from Canada shared their on-ground experiences, fears, and hopes. As he typed away, Alan felt a renewed sense of purpose, realizing he wasn't alone in his quest for understanding and change.

Alan's return to the digital space wasn't solely a passive endeavor. The more he interacted with the online community, the more he felt a sense of urgency. Recognizing the potential of a united front, he proposed the idea of a formal society. While online forums were efficient for discussions, Alan believed that a structured collaboration was necessary to bring about tangible change. His suggestion garnered significant support, and soon an online meeting was set, inviting participants from different provinces to discuss the way forward. The meeting was scheduled on a secure platform, ensuring the safety and privacy of its participants. The atmosphere was charged with anticipation as attendees logged in, their geographical locations spanning the width and breadth of Canada.

As the meeting kicked off, members began introducing themselves, discussing their backgrounds, experiences, and motivations. It became evident that the society was a mosaic of diverse skill sets: there were researchers, grassroots activists, tech professionals, educators, and even government insiders. They delved deep into discussions about resources at hand, potential challenges, and strategized the best way to leverage their collective strength. Some talked about their local networks, others about their digital expertise, and a few even mentioned financial resources they were willing to contribute. The exchange was a testament to the incredible potential that lay in collaboration, with each individual adding a unique piece to the puzzle.

Throughout the discussions, Alan's natural leadership qualities shone brightly. He was adept at steering conversations, ensuring every voice was heard, and synthesizing ideas into actionable plans. His knack for spotting synergies and connecting members with complementary skills was particularly notable. There was a gravitas about him, a calm assurance that inspired confidence. As the hours went by, it was evident to all present that this society was more than just a fleeting online endeavor. Under Alan's guidance, it was rapidly evolving into a formidable movement, driven by shared goals and mutual respect.

The formation of a new society, especially one with such significant stakes, required strategic planning and delegation. Every individual who chose to be a part of this endeavor needed to recognize their strengths and put them to use. The diverse backgrounds and expertise of the members made it easier for roles to organically fall into place. Some members, with backgrounds in media and communication, willingly took up roles in public relations, readying themselves to shape the society's public image. On the other hand, those proficient in the digital space stepped up for cybersecurity, fully aware of the online threats and cyber-espionage they might face given the nature of their cause. It was a spectrum of talent, from outreach coordinators to logistical experts, all ready to pour their efforts into the True North Society.

Settling on a name had been a process of consideration and debate, but when "The True North Society" was proposed, there was an almost unanimous agreement. The name evoked a sense of purpose, direction, and pride; it held within it the essence of Canada, its values, and its compass always pointing to what's right. There was a palpable enthusiasm in the virtual room when the name was chosen. It was not just about picking a title but christening their journey, giving it identity and soul.

The technological angle Alan introduced was a game-changer. He presented innovative artificial intelligence software solutions and tools which would give them a distinct advantage in communications, data analysis, and mobilization. His role was pivotal, offering not just tech-based solutions but a vision for how technology could bolster their mission. Meanwhile, Chantal, always Alan's biggest cheerleader, was on cloud nine. She saw the potential of what they were building, and the fire in Alan's eyes only fuelled her excitement. Her support was unwavering, and her belief in the cause and in Alan's capabilities added a layer of determination to the budding society. She wasn't just an observer; she was a pillar of strength, ready to play her part in this ambitious endeavor.

They scheduled a meeting for the following week. Amidst the soft blue glow of computer screens, members of the True North Society logged into a virtual conference room from various corners of Canada. The atmosphere was electric with anticipation, each attendee represented by an icon on a digital map spanning the vast Canadian expanse.

Alan's face appeared crisply on the shared screen. "Good evening, everyone," he began with an energy that instantly captivated the room. "Tonight, I want to unveil a vision—a transformative path for Canada."

As the presentation graphics rolled, he dove in. "The GlobeTrotter Ecosystem. More than just a concept, it's the key to our renewed, resilient Canada." He explained the innovative foundation of this ecosystem. "Built upon an immutable blockchain, powered and optimized by cutting-edge artificial intelligence, every transaction and decision made will be transparent and viewable. A technology that champions our Canadian values."

Attendees leaned in closer to their screens. "This isn't just an economic model," Alan continued. "It's a social reform. It integrates a direct voting system, granting every citizen an active role in shaping our nation's destiny. Every voice will be heard, every vote will count."

A sense of empowerment began to swell within the digital gathering. Alan, sensing the momentum, pressed on. "Companies can no longer hide in the shadows of ambiguity. Tax evasion, backroom deals, and corruption will be things of the past. The GlobeTrotter Ecosystem ensures everyone, from conglomerates, to governments, to individuals, operate within the same transparent, fair parameters."

Pausing momentarily to let the implications sink in, he added, "While organizations like the World Economic Forum have their vision for the globe, our ecosystem stands distinct. It's not about a centralized power dictating our fate. It's about giving power back to the people. The GlobeTrotter Ecosystem is the antithesis of what they propose."

The virtual room was charged with a collective zeal. Comments flooded in — "Revolutionary!", "A true game-changer!", "Canada will lead once more!"

Alan concluded, "With GlobeTrotter, we're not merely dreaming of a brighter future. We're constructing it, block by immutable block. Let's rebuild Canada — stronger, fairer, and truer to our values."

The affirmation and support that streamed in from across the nation echoed a unanimous sentiment: The GlobeTrotter Ecosystem was not just a proposal, but a beacon of hope for Canada's future.

Chapter 6

Building Bridges

The inception of the True North Society required not just internal structuring but also external outreach. Alan, ever the strategist, understood that to bring real change, they needed voices that resonated far and wide. With this in mind, the society, after hours of research and discussion, curated a list of influential figures who could champion their cause. Among the names were individuals like Jordan Peterson, known for his intellectual prowess and global reach. Joe Rogan, with his expansive platform that touched millions daily, and Alex Neve, a human rights advocate known for his compelling narratives on justice and change. These were individuals who not only held clout but also had a track record of challenging status quo and being the harbingers of change.

The society's approach to these influential figures had to be meticulously planned. Given the stature and busy schedules of these individuals, a standard outreach wouldn't suffice. They needed a blend of the personal and the professional. For some, face-to-face meetings were prioritized. Alan believed that sitting across a table, looking into the eyes of these figures, and sharing the vision of the society could strike a more profound chord. Personal letters were also a part of their arsenal. Crafted with care and precision, these letters not only laid out the objectives of the True North Society but also evoked emotion, ensuring that the message hit home. They bore signatures of multiple society members, symbolizing unity and collective resolve.

Supplementing these traditional modes of contact were the digital campaigns, which were designed to pique interest and keep the engagement alive. Harnessing the power of social media platforms, the society-initiated hashtag campaigns, shared gripping visuals, and even teased interviews with some of their members. This blend of modern digital techniques with the age-old art of personal connection ensured that their outreach was both expansive and effective. They weren't just sending out messages; they were building bridges with those who could amplify their mission.

As the True North Society started its ambitious outreach, they were met with a mosaic of reactions, painting a diverse, sometimes challenging picture of their road ahead. Some influencers, perhaps due to their own affiliations or busy schedules, were quick to dismiss the society's endeavors, considering them to be just another group with lofty ambitions and little substance. These dismissals, while disheartening, were not entirely unexpected. In the vast world of activism, many voices vied for attention, and skepticism often served as a protective barrier against the cacophony.

Then there were those who, while not immediately dismissive, showcased a palpable curiosity. They replied with probing questions, trying to understand the depth of the society's objectives and the validity of their methods. These influencers, while not allies off the bat, provided the society with an opportunity, a window to further explain their vision and hopefully, win them over. Such interactions often involved lengthy email threads, video calls, and sometimes, second and third meetings. Every query, every raised eyebrow was an opportunity for Alan and his team to refine their pitch, to learn, and to grow.

Amongst these interactions, a pivotal moment arose when Alan secured a meeting with a well-respected journalist known for his incisive articles and broad readership. Their initial conversation was supposed to last a mere thirty minutes but extended into hours. As Alan laid out the society's mission, the journalist, initially reserved, slowly became more engaged, nodding in agreement, and offering insights from his own experiences. By the end of their conversation, it was clear that the True North Society had found more than just a passive supporter—they had found a game-changing ally. This journalist not only promised to cover their activities but also became instrumental in introducing them to other potential supporters in the media realm. The tides were turning, and with each new ally, the society's dreams seemed more and more attainable.

True North Society Mission Statement

In the face of rapid societal shifts and political uncertainty, the True North Society stands as a beacon of unity, understanding, and forward-thinking action. We are a collective of dedicated individuals from all walks of life, spanning the vast and diverse landscape of Canada. Our mission is threefold:

1. **Unity in Diversity:** We aim to bridge the divides that have grown between communities, emphasizing that while we may have our differences, we share common dreams, aspirations, and values. By fostering conversations and creating platforms for dialogue, we strive to bring Canadians together, reminding one and all of the strength inherent in our mosaic.

2. **Informed Action:** We believe that change is not only inevitable but essential for growth. However, this change must be guided by well-informed decisions, deep understanding, and a commitment to the collective good. Through outreach, education, and partnerships, we advocate for policies and initiatives that reflect the best interests of all Canadians.

3. **Innovation for Tomorrow:** Recognizing the rapidly changing global landscape, we champion the integration of innovative technologies and ideas in addressing Canada's challenges. By staying at the forefront of technological advancements, we ensure that our nation is not just keeping pace with the world but leading the way in creating a brighter, more sustainable future.

In essence, the True North Society is more than just a coalition; it's a movement. A movement to reclaim the spirit of 'True North, strong and free,' ensuring that Canada's legacy is one of unity, progress, and enduring hope.

As weeks turned into months, the True North Society experienced a surge in membership, with prominent figures from various sectors stepping forth. Among these were celebrated academics, renowned artists, successful business magnates, and even some former politicians who felt the country's current direction had strayed from its core values. Their inclusion was more than symbolic; they brought with them not only their vast networks but resources that significantly bolstered the society's operations. The society's weekly virtual meetings, which initially saw around a dozen participants, swelled to hundreds. The diversity of expertise and perspective in these sessions was palpable, leading to more comprehensive strategies and initiatives.

Public awareness of the True North Society skyrocketed, in part due to media coverage but also because of its grassroots engagement. Volunteers would set up information booths in public spaces, from university campuses to weekend farmer markets, sparking conversations with passersby about the future of Canada. Personal stories were shared – of worries, hopes, and dreams – forming a tapestry of Canadian aspirations. The society's message of unity in diversity, informed action, and innovation resonated deeply with these narratives, drawing more to their cause. The society's digital campaigns went viral, with hashtags related to their mission trending on Canadian social media platforms. Their YouTube channel, featuring thoughtfully produced videos on various topics, gathered a significant following.

However, it was the series of town hall meetings that cemented the society's growing influence. Organized in cities and towns across Canada, these gatherings became a testament to the burgeoning movement's reach. From the bustling streets of Toronto to the quiet communities in the Yukon, Canadians came out in large numbers, eager to participate in these discussions. Each town hall became an occasion for introspection and forward-thinking, as community leaders, alongside society members, facilitated debates, workshops, and brainstorming sessions. Through these platforms, it became increasingly evident that the society's message wasn't just a resonating echo but a clarion call, inspiring Canadians to come together for a shared vision.

Alan, as an inventor and innovator, had always been an advocate for change and innovation. In a pivotal meeting with members of the True North Society, he unveiled the design of the GlobeTrotter Ecosystem, Alan's enthusiasm was palpable. He passionately explained the core objective: to build a world devoid of corruption, power abuses, poverty, and government overreach. The foundation of this ecosystem was uniquely solidified by incorporating the best aspects of all known ideologies, ensuring only the most positive components were retained. By instating a world where every vote mattered, and essential commodities were always within reach, Alan envisioned a brighter, fairer future for all.

The members of the society were excited. The details of the GlobeTrotter Ecosystem presented a fresh and radical approach to tackling systemic issues. The concept of Universal Basic Income and Jobs (UBIJ) was particularly appealing. By ensuring every adult and young adult around the globe a guaranteed income, independent of government or individual interference, it offered a tangible solution to persistent problems like poverty and inequality. As Alan delved deeper into the mechanism of the new digital currency uncontrolled by any government or person, and its operation on a hybrid blockchain, the members could see the potential. A currency that guaranteed security and speed, devoid of the pitfalls of excessive power consumption, and a UBIJ system that made certain everyone had a basic income irrespective of the government's fiscal health.

Alan emphasized, with an urgency in his voice, that the GlobeTrotter Ecosystem wasn't just about a financial overhaul. It aimed for a comprehensive reform across all systems and industries. The stock markets, educational and healthcare systems, the food & beverage industry, manufacturing, and service sectors were all poised for a transformation. Even areas like transportation, mental well-being, cultural preservation, and digital privacy weren't left out. The Ecosystem proposed a new legal system and a complete redesign of how ethics within artificial intelligence functioned. It was clear that the intention was to not just touch upon, but thoroughly reshape, every facet of society, creating an interconnected and transparent system where industries collaborated for the greater good.

Yet, with every revolutionary idea comes the challenge of implementation. Many questions arose. How would this system reshape Canadian society? Would it offer a potent counter to the existing government's corruption and avarice? Discussions flowed, and members began to see how the GlobeTrotter Ecosystem could level the playing field, diminishing, and even eliminating, the might of the elites. The potential to prepare for the impact of automation and AI, which threatened job losses, was especially salient. But more than the technicalities, it was the vision of a world where businesses were taxed justly, where inflation was eliminated, and where financial power was redistributed that resonated deeply. For the True North Society, Alan's GlobeTrotter Ecosystem wasn't just a blueprint; it symbolized hope.

Chapter 7

Resistance

From the grand chambers of the parliament to the private offices of bureaucrats, the government's initial response to the True North Society was a calculated display of apathy. They wielded their words like weapons, aiming to diminish the society's credibility in the eyes of the general populace. Instead of addressing the objectives head-on, government officials adopted a strategy of reduction. They repeatedly referred to the True North Society as a "fringe group," their ideas nothing more than wishful thinking that lacked the depth and understanding of the intricacies of governance and international diplomacy. There was a stark contrast between the hopes and aspirations of the society's members and the way they were depicted in official statements. The government's portrayal was of a group that posed a threat to the stability of the nation, individuals who couldn't appreciate the bigger picture, and were naive in their understanding of global dynamics.

Press conferences became stages for theatrical performances of righteous indignation. Government spokespeople, polished and poised, stood behind their podiums, expressing their deep concern for the direction in which such 'agitations' could lead the country. They painted a narrative that was hard for many to question: the nation was stable, thriving, and on a path to greatness, and any assertion otherwise was merely the disgruntled noise of a few. "We value every voice," one spokesperson mentioned in a press conference, "but we cannot allow misinformation and baseless claims to divert us from our path of progress." The term "agitators" was thrown around liberally, a label designed to delegitimize any form of dissent. The conferences seemed less about addressing concerns and more about convincing the public that there was no smoke, no fire, and certainly no cause for alarm.

Yet, beneath the dismissive exterior, there were subtle signs that the government was more concerned than they let on. Closed-door meetings increased, alliances were checked and double-checked, and surveillance on the society members grew more rigorous. There was a palpable tension, a sense that while the surface remained calm, beneath ran currents of anxiety and apprehension. The True North Society was gaining traction, and the government, despite its public display of nonchalance, was taking notice.

The shadows of whispers began subtly. They were carefully crafted snippets of stories, designed with just enough vagueness to invite questions. However, as days passed, these whispers morphed into roaring allegations, filling columns of newspapers, dominating television news segments, and rapidly spreading through social media channels. A methodical campaign aimed at undermining Alan's credibility was in full swing. It was evident that those who felt threatened by the True North Society's objectives and Alan's leadership were resorting to old tactics: character assassination. The GlobeTrotter Ecosystem, with its revolutionary vision, was gaining attention, and in response, the establishment sought to break its most vocal advocate.

One morning, a reputed national daily featured an explosive article on its front page. The headline screamed allegations about Alan's questionable past. It delved into intricate details, twisting, and turning facts to depict a narrative of a man with dubious intentions. The article was particularly scathing, portraying him as someone who had a track record of disputes and disagreements. It highlighted minor fallouts with past employers, exaggerating them to look like full-blown vendettas. The intention was clear: paint Alan as a serial troublemaker, a person driven by personal grudges rather than genuine concern for society. Quoting unnamed sources, the article even hinted at several scandalous activities, carefully crafted to put his character into question. The media, sensing a sensational story, lapped it up, and soon the narrative was everywhere.

In the face of overwhelming media scrutiny, Alan chose to address the issue head-on. During a press conference organized by the True North Society, he stood tall, a figure of defiance against the swirling storm of accusations. With calm determination, he began to narrate his side of the story. "It's true," he began, "I've always had an intense aversion to bullies, to the corrupt, to those who use power for personal gain." He went on to detail the instances from his past where he had taken matters into his own hands, confronting individuals and organizations that exemplified tyranny and corruption. While some of his actions might have been on the boundaries of legality, they were always against those who epitomized injustice. "I was young, brash, and perhaps not always right in my methods. But my heart was in the right place." He admitted. As he spoke, it became evident that the very traits that were being criticized were the ones that made him the passionate leader of a movement for change. He concluded, "Yes, there might have been better ways, but in the face of injustice, I chose action over silence."

The atmosphere was palpable inside the meeting room, where members of the True North Society had gathered. The recent barrage of media attacks on Alan had left many feeling concerned, but also even more resolute. Elder members and newcomers alike sat shoulder to shoulder, a sea of faces with a shared purpose. There was an unmistakable determination in the air. As the meeting commenced, one by one, members began to express their unwavering support for Alan. Maria, a university professor from Quebec, spoke passionately about how she'd witnessed Alan's dedication to the cause firsthand. "I've seen Alan's commitment. These attacks only further prove the righteousness of our path. We must rally behind him now more than ever," she urged. Jatin, a tech expert from Vancouver, emphasized the importance of unity. "We knew this wouldn't be easy. They're trying to break us apart, but we stand united." These sentiments were echoed throughout the room, as many shared personal anecdotes of Alan's integrity and their belief in the society's goals.

As the show of support continued, the conversation naturally progressed to discussing strategies to counteract the smearing tactics deployed by the government and certain media outlets. Chantal, utilizing her vast network, suggested organizing public talks and workshops that could serve to educate the general public about the GlobeTrotter Ecosystem and the society's objectives. "We need to ensure our message isn't drowned in the sea of disinformation," she remarked. Marcus, a digital marketing expert, proposed the idea of an online campaign, flooding all platforms with authentic stories of society members, focusing on the positive changes the GlobeTrotter Ecosystem could bring. "Let's take control of the narrative. Let the truth be our strongest weapon," he emphasized. The room buzzed with ideas, from producing documentaries to harnessing the power of influencers who believed in their cause. The society was gearing up to ensure their vision wasn't tainted by the government's propaganda.

As days progressed, social media was abuzz with a new sentiment. Everywhere, posts began to emerge, pointing out the glaring irony of the government's stance towards the True North Society. "If the society was as inconsequential as the government claims," wrote one Twitter user, "why the need for such an aggressive disinformation campaign?" Another post on Instagram showcased a side-by-side comparison of the society's mission and the government's counterclaims, highlighting the stark discrepancies. Memes began to flood the internet, with captions like "Scared much?" and "Why so obsessed with us?" Many Canadians started to see through the thin veil of the government's tactics, realizing that if they weren't threatened by the society's potential, they wouldn't be dedicating so much effort to discredit them. The digital realm was awash with the sentiment that the very resistance they were facing was, in fact, a testament to the society's growing influence.

The city streets buzzed with chatter as local media took to interviewing average Canadians. Standing at a busy intersection in downtown Toronto, a young journalist approached a middle-aged woman carrying groceries.

The question was simple, "What do you think of the True North Society and their objectives?" The woman paused for a moment, adjusting her glasses, "Look, I've lived through enough governments and promises to know that they rarely get things right. The society? At least they're offering something different. A change. Can't be worse than what we've got now, can it?" Not far away, a college student with headphones dangling around his neck had a similar sentiment, "The government? Trust them? You're joking, right? All they've done is made a mess of things. This society though, they're sparking hope. That's more than I can say for our so-called leaders." However, it wasn't all positive. An older gentleman, puffing on a cigar, scoffed at the very mention of the society. "They think they can change the world with some grand plan? Please. It's all talk." Yet, even amid the dissent, a common thread emerged—discontentment with the status quo and a yearning for change.

In neighborhoods, community centers, and even online, the society's supporters became more vocal and proactive. They organized meetups, townhall sessions, and started grassroots campaigns, aimed not just at promoting the society's agenda, but also defending Alan's reputation against the mudslinging. Sarah, a retired school teacher, decided to share her personal encounter with Alan in a heartfelt video. "I met Alan at a conference his mother held years ago. Even back then, his passion for justice and his desire to create a fairer society was evident. These accusations? They're just attempts to tarnish the reputation of someone genuinely trying to make a difference." Her video went viral, gathering thousands of shares and comments. On campuses, students set up information booths, distributing pamphlets about the society's objectives and holding Q&A sessions to clear doubts. Photos of Alan working alongside society members, helping in community projects, and engaging in charitable activities began to flood social media, all aimed at painting a true picture of the man behind the vision.

But perhaps the most touching were the stories from those who had known Alan on a personal level. Long lost friends, ex-colleagues, even acquaintances from his school days stepped forward to share anecdotes that showcased his character. They painted a picture of a man who, even in his youth, stood up against bullies and always defended the underdog. "I remember when we were in high school," one friend recalled, "Alan intervened when a group was picking on a new immigrant student. He got a black eye for his troubles, but he said it was worth it." These tales showcased not just Alan's passion for justice, but his willingness to act, even at personal cost. As these stories spread, they began to counteract the negative press, with many Canadians openly questioning the authenticity of the fabricated scandals against him. The grassroots campaigns served as a reminder of the strength of community and genuine testimonies in shaping public perception.

Chapter 8

The Innovation

Tucked away in the heart of Piedmont in the Laurentians, in his workshop of unassuming brick and stone, lay Alan's office. The entrance opened to a space that was nothing short of an inventor's dream. The room felt alive, almost like the pulsating heart of innovation. Shelves lined the walls, filled with prototypes of his earlier inventions, each carrying its own tale of trials, failures, successes, and lessons. Some were mechanical wonders, while others harnessed cutting-edge technology. Some appeared simple in design yet had profound implications in their application. Every device, every model, was a testament to Alan's relentless spirit of invention. Interwoven among these artifacts of his inventive prowess were sketches and blueprints of projects still in their infancy—innovations that promised to redefine boundaries.

Nestled amidst these symbols of the past and future were antiques that added an unexpected charm to the environment. A vintage gramophone stood proudly on a wooden table, its brass horn gleaming under the warm light of a nearby lamp. There was a classic typewriter, its keys well-worn from use, perhaps a nod to the age when ideas were meticulously hammered onto paper. A beautiful painting of a cowboy with a Coke that his sister had painted. A beautifully crafted wooden globe from the 19th century sat on his desk, an ode to exploration, and perhaps, a metaphorical nod to the GlobeTrotter Ecosystem he was so passionately building.

In the midst of all this, Alan could often be found hunched over his workspace, deeply engrossed in his theoretical GlobeTrotter Ecosystem. The sheer complexity of introducing such a radical shift in the global economic structure meant that every detail, every nuance had to be accounted for. To help him in this Herculean task, Alan employed state-of-the-art artificial intelligence systems. Multiple monitors displayed various simulations, algorithms, and models, all driven by AI. This AI was designed to challenge, test, and refine every facet of the GlobeTrotter blueprint. It would raise questions, expose potential weaknesses, and even propose solutions. Alan would often be seen in deep conversations with his digital assistant, sometimes in agreement, other times in intense debate. It was a dance of human ingenuity and machine precision, each pushing the other to their limits, each refining the other. This synergy was not just about creating a flawless system on paper; it was about ensuring that the GlobeTrotter Ecosystem was resilient, robust, and ready to usher in a new era for humanity.

Alan, with his profound understanding of systems and the dynamics of change, knew that for the GlobeTrotter Ecosystem to stand the test of reality, it had to be poked, prodded, and examined from every conceivable angle. To achieve this, he tapped into the wealth of knowledge that resided within the coalition. Among its members were economists, financial analysts, sociologists, and experts in various fields. Alan sought them out, organizing focused meetings to dissect, debate, and refine the ecosystem's every facet. These were not just sessions where they examined numbers or trends. Instead, they delved into the very core of societal dynamics, understanding how the proposed changes would ripple across communities, regions, and eventually, the globe. As days turned into nights, countless scenarios were laid out, scrutinized, and optimized, ensuring that the GlobeTrotter Ecosystem was as resilient and foolproof as humanly possible.

The office space that once seemed like a reflection of Alan's mind turned into a hive of activity during these late-night brainstorming sessions. Large whiteboards were strewn with equations, flowcharts, and notes. The camera and monitor on the opposite wall for all the people online to see. Diagrams detailed the interplay between various components of the ecosystem, helping the team visualize the vast network they were crafting. As the evening sky darkened, the room was illuminated only by the soft glow of desk lamps and the fervor of ideas igniting. Cups of coffee, half-eaten sandwiches, and stacks of reference books littered the space, bearing testimony to the relentless drive of the team. The atmosphere was thick with intensity—every minute, every second was precious. The pressure of time weighed heavily, but it was counteracted by an equally strong force: passion. Each member was driven not just by the enormity of the task but by the sheer potential of the change they were about to usher in.

Yet, these sessions were not all about work. Amid the deep dives and intense debates, there were moments of camaraderie and levity. Someone would share an anecdote, a joke, or a story, lightening the mood. Laughter would ring out, reminding everyone that while the task at hand was serious, the journey itself was to be cherished. These interludes were essential, recharging the team's spirits, and reinforcing the bonds between them. After all, they were not just colleagues working on a project; they were visionaries, united by a shared dream, shaping a brighter future for all of humanity.

As days turned into nights and nights into days, Alan's workspace became a hive of activity, drawing in technologists, economists, and software developers. Together, they began to meticulously construct the backbone of the GlobeTrotter Ecosystem: a state-of-the-art blockchain powered by cutting-edge artificial intelligence. This wasn't just any blockchain, but one meticulously designed to handle a revolutionary voting system, ensuring every voice was truly heard. They developed a new currency, symbolic of the ecosystem's aspirations, and a variety of tokens, each tailored for specific uses within the system. The smartphone wallet was designed to be user-friendly, ensuring that people from all walks of life could easily access and manage their funds, while a sophisticated smart contracts system was implemented to ensure transparency and trustworthiness in transactions. And at the heart of it all was the Universal Basic Income system, a beacon of hope and equality, ensuring every individual was catered for. The synergy of these elements symbolized not just technological advancement but a dream of a brighter, fairer future.

A quaint community nestled in the picturesque region of Quebec was carefully selected as the initial testbed for the GlobeTrotter Ecosystem. The community, with its mix of urban and rural elements, was deemed the ideal representative of Canadian society at large. It possessed the necessary infrastructure to facilitate the implementation and yet retained the simplicity and close-knit nature characteristic of smaller communities. Before launching, Alan and his team met with community leaders, briefed them about the process, and laid out a roadmap. Instead of thrusting the entire system upon the people all at once, a phased approach was decided upon. Every week, a different aspect of the GlobeTrotter Ecosystem would be introduced, ensuring a smooth and gradual transition, allowing the community to adapt and provide feedback at each step.

With the first week's roll-out, the changes were subtle but significant. Local businesses began aligning their operations with the new system, and community members started experiencing the initial shifts in economic dynamics. The most visible change, however, was the palpable sense of excitement in the air. People felt they were part of a grand experiment, a potential solution to the world's multifaceted problems. As weeks progressed, more layers of the ecosystem were unveiled, from the implementation of the new tax system to the redistribution of resources. Each stage was meticulously monitored by Alan's team, collecting data, observing behavior patterns, and assimilating feedback. Community town halls became regular events, where people would gather, share their experiences, and voice their suggestions or concerns.

The initial feedback surpassed even the most optimistic expectations. The community not only embraced the changes but became its most fervent advocates. Small business owners reported an uptick in their profits, while households felt a palpable relief from financial strains. Youth, who were often the most resistant to systemic changes, became the loudest champions of the GlobeTrotter Ecosystem. They felt empowered, seeing a future where their voices mattered and where opportunities weren't bottlenecked by antiquated systems. Local schools integrated the new economic concepts into their curriculum, ensuring the younger generation grew up understanding and appreciating the revolutionary changes happening around them. The trial was not without its challenges, but the overwhelming sentiment was clear: The GlobeTrotter Ecosystem, even in its infancy, had the potential to transform societies, and this small community in Quebec was living proof.

In the dimly lit boardroom, society members huddled together, pouring over maps, charts, and data, discussing the most effective way to unveil the GlobeTrotter Ecosystem to the public. The weight of what they had achieved weighed heavily upon them, and the anticipation of their nation's reaction was palpable. Rebecca, a communication strategist, emphasized the importance of a grassroots approach, "We need to start at the community level, engage the public directly, organize town hall sessions, and conduct workshops. This is how we build trust and debunk myths before they even arise." Simon, a media specialist, concurred, "Visibility is the key. We need to collaborate with journalists, influencers, and bloggers who can give us the reach, ensuring that the narrative remains in our control." Meanwhile, Helena, an educator in the group, proposed the initiation of a nationwide educational campaign. "We need to make sure every Canadian understands the core mechanics of this system, its advantages, and how it fundamentally differs from the existing one."

Tensions mounted as a sealed envelope made its way to Alan. The contents, a leaked memo, suggested that their efforts were not going unnoticed. The government, the very entity they aimed to reform, was deeply troubled by the prospects of the GlobeTrotter Ecosystem. As Alan read aloud, it became evident that the government viewed the system as a direct threat to its hegemony. The memo contained phrases like "urgent intervention required" and "strategies to mitigate mass adoption." The tone was unmistakably anxious, and the implications clear: the government recognized the potential of the GlobeTrotter Ecosystem and its capacity to disrupt the existing power structure. Maria, a lawyer in the society, highlighted, "This memo isn't just an acknowledgment of our work; it's a testament to its potency. They're scared because they understand the true ramifications of the ecosystem."

As members absorbed the contents of the memo, their focus shifted from mere introduction to safeguarding the system. Strategies to protect the GlobeTrotter Ecosystem from potential governmental intervention or sabotage became the topic of fervent discussion. Some proposed the creation of a decentralized backup system to ensure that even if one part of the network was targeted, the ecosystem would continue to function. Others suggested liaising with international allies and organizations that championed similar causes to build a global shield of support. Alan, ever the visionary, summarized the mood, "The fact that they're concerned validates our efforts. But we have to be smart, agile, and united. Their resistance is a testament to the change we're about to bring. Let's ensure that the GlobeTrotter Ecosystem, built on the principles of equality, transparency, and decentralization, is not just introduced but becomes an indomitable force for good in Canada and beyond."

In a moment of profound clarity, Alan declared, "For the GlobeTrotter Ecosystem to be our enduring legacy, we'll build a hybrid blockchain—a fortress of technology that remains impregnable. Not just resilient, but impossible to hack. This was our original vision, and while we didn't need it for the trial, it's imperative for the system's global implementation and security."

Chapter 9

Rising Tide

The atmosphere in the grand hall was electrifying. Spotlights streamed down onto the stage, illuminating a backdrop of a massive blue and white globe—the emblem of GlobeTrotter. Rows upon rows of seats filled with a sea of faces representing a cross-section of society: from journalists scribbling hurried notes to tech enthusiasts, influencers capturing every moment, and community leaders nodding in contemplative approval. It was evident that this wasn't just an event; it was a turning point in history.

The venue was chosen with care—a symbolic location that merged the modern with the traditional, reflecting GlobeTrotter's vision of integrating innovative solutions with time-honored principles. Large screens were strategically placed, ensuring that everyone had a clear view of the stage. The air buzzed with anticipation as whispers and murmurs filled the room, speculating on what would be unveiled.

As the clock ticked closer to the start time, a montage played, showing glimpses of the trials in Quebec, the late-night brainstorming sessions, and the determination of the society members. The soundtrack was a symphony of hope, echoing the aspirations and dreams of millions. By the end of the montage, there was hardly a dry eye in the room. The emotional weight was palpable, setting the stage for what was to come.

Stepping onto the stage, Alan took a moment to gaze out into the crowd, his eyes reflecting a mixture of determination, hope, and vulnerability. Clearing his throat, he began, "Good evening, everyone. Today marks not just a new chapter for Canada, but potentially, a new chapter for humanity."

"The path that led us to this juncture was paved with challenges, doubt, and resistance. Yet, at every step, we've been driven by a singular vision: a world where every individual's voice counts, where essential needs are met, and where the corrupt and greedy can't exploit the system. The GlobeTrotter Ecosystem, born out of dissecting all known ideologies, and meticulously extracting only their positive facets—acknowledging that each ideology was initially conceived to serve humanity but had elements that inadvertently worked against the people—stands as a testament to our dedication. The GlobeTrotter Ecosystem isn't just a theoretical concept; it's a testament to what we can achieve when we unite for a common purpose."

Drawing a deep breath, he continued, "As we stand here, on the precipice of change, I want you all to understand that GlobeTrotter isn't my brainchild alone. It's the result of countless hours spent by a coalition of dedicated individuals, and the input of communities like the one in Quebec. It's built on the hopes of every individual who dreams of a better world. Tonight, we present to Canada—and to the world—a system that champions transparency, equality, and decentralization. A system that offers a fair playing field for all, where power isn't concentrated in the hands of a few, but distributed equally among the many."

Continuing his speech with conviction, Alan declared, "The GlobeTrotter Ecosystem isn't just an innovation; it's a revolution. Together, let's embark on this journey towards a brighter, more equitable future. The tide is rising, and it's up to us to ride the wave. Thank you." The hall erupted in applause, resonating with the hope and promise of a new dawn.

Alan took a brief moment, letting the applause settle, before continuing with a fire of passion in his eyes. "Now, let's delve into the heart of the GlobeTrotter Ecosystem and its profound potential to reshape our world."

"In a world where misinformation is rampant and where a significant portion of the population feels unheard, the GlobeTrotter Ecosystem promises transparency. No more hidden agendas or backdoor deals. Every decision, every transaction, every detail will be recorded on our hybrid blockchain, ensuring that data is verifiable, immutable, and, most importantly, transparent to all. This isn't just about technology; it's about trust—trust in systems, trust in governance, trust in each other."

He shifted his weight and leaned forward slightly, as if sharing a secret. "Economic disparities and inequalities have long plagued our societies. How many dreams have been stifled because of lack of resources? How many potential leaders have we lost to the cycle of poverty? With GlobeTrotter, we're introducing a Universal Basic Income system, ensuring that everyone starts on a level playing field. Our unique digital currency, combined with a thoughtful token system, decentralizes economic power, ensuring that wealth isn't hoarded, but rather, is circulated, invested, shared, and most importantly, not controlled by anyone but yourselves. Plus, there would no longer be personal income taxes for anyone!" The Crowd cheered!

As Alan continued, he painted a vivid picture of the challenges that the GlobeTrotter Ecosystem seeks to address. "Our current systems are often one sided towards the rich and powerful, cumbersome, inaccessible, and exclusionary. Contracts and laws that are meant to safeguard us often become tools of exploitation because of their complexity. GlobeTrotter's smart contract system is here to change that—making contracts transparent, accessible, and genuinely beneficial for all parties involved. And, with our smartphone wallet, financial empowerment is literally at the fingertips of every individual."

Pausing, Alan scanned the room, ensuring that every word found its mark. "Lastly, let's address the elephants in the room—corruption. How many times have we felt the sting of betrayal by those meant to serve us? The GlobeTrotter Ecosystem doesn't just seek to reduce corruption; it seeks to eliminate it. Corporate tax evasion? No more! Companies will no longer be able to hide their money. Our AI-driven voting system ensures every voice is heard, every vote is counted, and every decision is in the best interest of the collective."

He concluded with a note of optimism, "GlobeTrotter isn't just about countering problems; it's about crafting solutions. Solutions that don't just benefit the privileged few but uplift every individual. Solutions that promise a brighter, more inclusive future. Together, let's make that future a reality." A thunderous ovation echoed through the place.

The GlobeTrotter Ecosystem's launch didn't merely ripple through the community—it created a tidal wave. Within hours of Alan's speech, major online platforms were inundated with chatter. Canadians from all walks of life took to social media, expressing their awe, opinions, hopes, and questions. Hashtags like #GlobeTrotterFuture, #AlanSpeaksTruth, and #EcosystemRevolution trended not just nationally, but even started making rounds globally. Influential bloggers and vloggers began dissecting every aspect of the ecosystem, resulting in videos with millions of views. It was clear; the GlobeTrotter Ecosystem had captured the collective imagination, turning even the most apathetic individuals into fervent discussants.

With interest soaring, the society was quick to respond to the public's thirst for knowledge. They set up a series of online webinars, aiming to break down the intricacies of the GlobeTrotter Ecosystem. These weren't mere presentations; they were interactive sessions, where attendees could get answers directly from experts within the society. The coalition's economy-savvy members, including Alan, took turns hosting, ensuring participants got in-depth and diverse perspectives. Topics ranged from the blockchain's security aspects to the principles underpinning the UBI system. It wasn't long before these sessions became a must-attend, attracting tens of thousands from across Canada and even globally. Furthermore, to keep the conversation going, the society launched a dedicated forum, allowing Canadians to share their insights, stories, and aspirations linked to the GlobeTrotter Ecosystem.

The tidal wave of enthusiasm didn't stop at Canada's borders; it resonated across continents. The world had been intently watching, and what they saw inspired a universal yearning for change. Nations from every corner of the globe, from the bustling cities of Europe to the expansive landscapes of Africa, from the dense urban centers of Asia to the lively towns of South America, were eager to adopt the GlobeTrotter Ecosystem. This wasn't just about replication; it was about embracing a system that, by design, catered to a universal set of human aspirations and needs.

What was striking was the inherent adaptability of the GlobeTrotter Ecosystem. Even though it was a global system, its features resonated with local communities everywhere. People recognized its potential to address not only systemic corruption and inefficiencies but also to empower individual citizens, ensuring that each voice was heard and valued. This was more than just technology; it was a philosophy, a new social contract being forged in the digital age.

International media buzzed with stories of nations making swift strides towards adopting the GlobeTrotter Ecosystem. Forums, conferences, and conventions were organized worldwide, fostering a sense of shared commitment and vision. As more and more countries embraced Alan's innovation, it became evident that a new chapter in global solidarity and cooperative progress was being written. The GlobeTrotter Ecosystem was not just a Canadian marvel; it was a gift to the world, promising a brighter, interconnected future for all.

Within the solemn halls of Ottawa, a palpable tension filled the air. The GlobeTrotter Ecosystem had surged in popularity, capturing the attention and hearts of Canadians from coast to coast. Emergency meetings were hastily convened within Trudeau's cabinet, an act that signified the significance of this novel entity. The normally composed corridors of the nation's capital buzzed with a blend of concern and astonishment. Cabinet members, seasoned in political maneuvers, found themselves grappling with an unexpected phenomenon.

Amidst the tall ceilings and the grandeur of the government buildings, unease permeated. Many officials, having underestimated the

GlobeTrotter Ecosystem, were now taken aback by its widespread embrace. Whispers filled the hallways, ranging from stunned inquiries about how such a transformative initiative could've quietly taken root to serious debates about its implications on the established political order. The mood was further compounded by a growing realization: The GlobeTrotter Ecosystem was not just a mere societal movement, but a formidable paradigm shift that was reshaping the nation's discourse.

While divisions began to surface within the cabinet, Justin Trudeau's stance was unmistakable. A combination of pride and a deeply rooted belief in his leadership ethos made the thought of collaborating with Alan inconceivable. To Trudeau, the GlobeTrotter Ecosystem, despite its merits and public appeal, was an affront to his administration's sovereignty. He believed that the integrity and supremacy of his government should remain uncontested. Within the cabinet, voices calling for diplomatic engagements and peaceful negotiations with Alan and the society were overshadowed by Trudeau's steadfast resolve. In his perspective, any concession or collaboration would not only signify weakness but also betray his inherent belief in the government's direction. This unwavering stance, fueled by his ego, set the stage for a looming standoff between the establishment and a society hungry for change.

In the quiet sanctuary of his personal office, amidst the hum of accolades and public attention, Alan found himself at the epicenter of a whirlwind of emotions. The GlobeTrotter Ecosystem was no longer a mere blueprint; it was a thriving reality, commanding the allegiance and aspirations of countless individuals. But as the din of external applause grew louder, an internal cacophony of questions and uncertainties besieged Alan. Was he genuinely pursuing this monumental task for the collective good of Canada and the broader world? Or had this become a quest to satiate his own ego, an arena for his personal glories and triumphs? He remembered the countless hours he had spent refining the system, and now, with the world watching, doubt gnawed at his convictions. Was he truly a selfless innovator or merely another ambitious individual masked under the guise of altruism?

Outside the room, the world celebrated the GlobeTrotter Ecosystem, but inside, shadows of doubt danced on the walls. As Alan grappled with these uncertainties, a gentle knock echoed through the room, heralding the arrival of Chantal. She had known Alan longer than most, having shared dreams, aspirations, and challenges alongside him. Observing the unease etched on his face, she softly began to speak. "Alan," she whispered, "this journey we've embarked upon was never solely about the destination, but the collective spirit of transformation and betterment." She reminded him of the countless nights they had spoken about a world devoid of corruption, greed, and exploitation—a world where the true essence of humanity flourished. Her words served as a bridge, connecting Alan to those cherished memories, the authentic vision they had aspired to create for the world. It wasn't about personal aggrandizement; it was about an age-old dream they had woven together.

Chantal's presence, like a lighthouse amidst a stormy sea, provided clarity and direction. She drew him out from the quagmire of doubts, allowing Alan to glimpse the bigger picture. "You've always spoken of a world where everyone has an equal chance, an environment where systems empower rather than suppress," she continued. "This isn't just about you or me. It's about generations to come, it's about the very essence of humanity striving for its best self." As her words washed over him, the weight on Alan's shoulders began to lift. The doubts that had momentarily clouded his vision dissipated, replaced by the reaffirmation of a mission greater than self. The journey ahead was challenging, but with allies like Chantal, the vision for a better world remained unwavering.

Chapter 10

In the Shadows

The flickering fluorescent lights in the underground government office barely provided any illumination, casting eerie, sporadic shadows over the room. The ambiance was tense, with the low murmur of intense discussions punctuated by the occasional shuffle of papers. Prime Minister Trudeau's silhouette was the most distinct, dominating the room. His tall frame paced back and forth impatiently; his face contorted in frustration. An uncharacteristic, almost petulant rage emanated from him. Those present could feel the palpable weight of his frustration, a rarity given his usual calm and measured demeanor.

The room was filled with some of the highest-ranking officials in the Canadian government. Yet, despite their collective power and influence, they all appeared wary, casting furtive glances at each other. Trudeau stopped pacing momentarily, placing both palms flat on the massive oak table, his fingers drumming anxiously. "This GlobeTrotter Ecosystem," he hissed, the anger evident in his voice, "is threatening the very foundations we've laid. How did this even happen under our watch? How did we let Alan gain such momentum?" The room was thick with tension, but none dared interrupt him or offer any solace.

Suddenly, Trudeau's eyes narrowed, a fleeting thought crossing his mind. He seemed momentarily lost, his gaze distant. "The Chinese," he murmured more to himself than anyone else, "how would they handle this? Perhaps there's a lesson to be learned from their efficiency." While it was no secret that Trudeau admired certain aspects of the Chinese governance model, hearing him vocalize it in such a precarious context made many officials uncomfortable. Yet, none voiced their concerns aloud, silently observing and waiting for his next directive.

The door to the office opened with a soft creak, revealing another shadowy figure. The newcomer handed over a manila envelope to one of the aides, who, in turn, placed it at the center of the table. The room's occupants leaned in; curiosity evident in their eyes. The envelope contained information on a covert operation, details on how to handle the ever-growing influence of Alan and the True North Society. As they leafed through the contents, whispers of the operation name, "Project Snowfall," floated around the room.

A middle-aged man, known to many as Director Langley, head of a discreet intelligence unit, took the floor. "Ladies and gentlemen," he began, his voice clear and commanding despite the room's dense atmosphere, "Project Snowfall is our answer to the GlobeTrotter challenge. It's an operation that focuses on close surveillance of Alan and every member of the society. Our primary objective is to monitor their movements, communications, and strategies closely." The room listened intently, hanging onto his every word.

Director Langley continued, "While surveillance is our primary goal, we must also be prepared to intervene and sabotage when necessary. We cannot, and I repeat, cannot allow the GlobeTrotter Ecosystem to gain any more traction. It's a threat to our establishment, our way of life." His stern expression conveyed the gravity of the situation. The room filled with nods of agreement. The stage was set. Project Snowfall was now in motion. The stakes had never been higher.

The quaint serenity of Alan's neighborhood, once a sanctuary for him, had lately taken on a more sinister undertone. On his morning jogs, where he once greeted familiar faces and exchanged pleasantries, he now observed unfamiliar figures that seemed to linger just a bit too long. They watched him with concealed interest, pretending to be engrossed in their newspapers or dog-walking routines, but Alan was not easily fooled. Their calculated moves and out-of-place attire were telltale signs that they weren't just ordinary residents or visitors. He knew he was being watched, but by whom and for what exact purpose remained unclear.

As days turned into weeks, the sense of being observed intensified. Outside his home, the occasional appearance of nondescript vans became frequent. These vehicles, with their tinted windows and missing license plates, would park at odd angles, attempting to blend in. Yet, their mere presence in such a tranquil neighborhood was anything but inconspicuous. Late into the night, Alan would sometimes spot shadows moving behind the van windows, and occasionally, the soft whirring sound of machinery. The realization was inescapable: they weren't just watching him; they were also likely intercepting his communications.

Alan's unease grew further when he began experiencing disruptions in his phone calls and internet connections. Video conferences with True North Society members were frequently interrupted, voices morphed into robotic sounds, and screen images distorted without reason. Alan knew he had to be more discreet and cautious. Opting for encrypted communication channels, he began using burner phones and changed his daily routines, ensuring that those tracking him would have a hard time predicting his next move. Though he was deeply entrenched in the mission of the GlobeTrotter Ecosystem, he knew he had to remain vigilant to protect himself and the society's vision.

Late one evening, while scrolling through his smartphone's Twitter app, a peculiar direct message notification popped up. The sender's account had no profile picture, and the username seemed a random jumble of letters and numbers. Hesitant but curious, Alan opened the message. It read: *"Alan, not everyone on the inside is against you. There are those among us who believe in what you're doing, who want to help the people genuinely. Tread carefully, but know that you have silent allies here. Trust no one fully, and always watch your back. #TheStormIsComing."* The message was cryptic, yet its intent seemed clear. Alan was taken aback; he'd always suspected that not every official was on board with suppressing the GlobeTrotter Ecosystem, but this was concrete proof. There was internal dissent within the government ranks, and this silent ally was risking a lot to send this warning.

Alan contemplated the meaning behind the hashtag and what the 'storm' could imply. The potential implications were vast and varied. However, it also gave him hope, knowing that there were those within the bureaucratic machinery who genuinely wanted positive change for the masses. With renewed determination, he realized the importance of his mission, not just for himself but for those silent voices within the government who couldn't openly support him. They were counting on him, just as much as the ordinary citizens hoping for a brighter future.

The True North Society's meetings were typically close-knit affairs, taking place in secret locations, known only to the inner circle. They were havens of trust and collaboration, free from external influences. However, one chilly evening, as Alan stood at the head of a wooden table surrounded by loyal members, a disturbance at the door caught everyone's attention. An unfamiliar figure, wrapped in a long trench coat with a hat pulled down, covering much of his face, tried to blend in with the crowd. Alan's eyes narrowed. He prided himself on knowing every face in the room, but this one was new and decidedly out of place. The stranger's nervous shuffling, furtive glances, and inability to maintain eye contact with anyone for more than a fleeting moment raised alarms in Alan's mind.

Using his sharp instincts, Alan calmly approached the individual, hoping to quell the palpable tension in the room. "Hello, friend. I don't believe we've met. What brings you to our gathering today?" Alan inquired, maintaining a facade of warmth. The intruder hesitated, eyes darting around as if searching for an escape route. "I, um, heard about your group and wanted to know more," the stranger stammered. But before he could offer further explanation, Alan, with an unexpected swift motion, reached out and tugged at the man's collar, revealing a discreet wire. The room went silent. The stranger's pale face turned a shade of crimson. "A government spy in our midst," Alan announced, his voice cold. Without another word, he grabbed the infiltrator by the scruff of his neck and, using his momentum, propelled him towards the exit, sending the spy tumbling out of the building onto the cold, hard ground.

The aftermath of the intrusion was a mix of disbelief and anger. Whispers of betrayal and shock permeated the room. But for Alan, this blatant infiltration attempt was both a validation and a warning. It confirmed that the government viewed the GlobeTrotter Ecosystem as a genuine threat, enough to warrant covert surveillance. Alan addressed the society members, "This intrusion makes it evident that we're on the right path. Our vision is so potent that those in power are scared. But we won't be deterred." His voice resonated with determination, "GlobeTrotter needs to be operational now more than ever. And as for Trudeau, it's clear that if Canada is to be saved, his reign needs to come to an end." The room filled with murmurs of agreement, and what had started as a typical society meeting transformed into a rallying cry. The stakes were higher, the opposition more formidable, but Alan's resolve to bring about change had only strengthened.

After a momentary pause, Alan locked eyes with each member present, his gaze intense and unwavering. "Listen to me," he began, his voice low but firm, "No matter what happens to me, you all have to promise me that you will move forward with this." He emphasized each word, ensuring the gravity of his request was felt by all. There was a unanimous nodding of heads, and a chorus of voices rose in agreement. "We promise, Alan," a member called out. Another chimed in, "We swear on it." One by one, society members made their pledge, sealing their commitment to the cause. The atmosphere was electric with unity, and the bonds among them, already strong, had been forged even tighter in that defining moment.

In the hushed meeting room, society members gathered, the atmosphere thick with a mix of tension and determination. Alan took center stage, gesturing to a few tech-savvy members to his side. He had always believed in being prepared, and in times like these, he knew the importance of keeping every conversation and every piece of information safe from prying eyes. "We cannot be naive enough to think we aren't being watched or listened to," he began, his tone urgent. "Every word we utter, every message we send, could be intercepted." With that, the team unveiled the encrypted communication tools they had been working on – cutting-edge software that would ensure their discussions remained private and untraceable. The members were given demonstrations on how to use these tools, from encrypted chat rooms to voice calls. Their commitment to protecting the mission was palpable.

Away from the tech and the screens, Alan found solace in his own kind of shield: nature. With every stone and wood beam, every tree and shrub, he had poured love and hope into building a house in the woods. Spanning 200 acres, it was a testament to Alan's foresight and his love for Chantal. Hidden from the modern world's hustle and bustle, this was Alan's sanctuary. He had dreamt that, someday, he and Chantal would share their lives there, away from city noise and close to the symphony of nature. The gentle hum of the forest, the babbling brooks, and the calls of the wild had always felt like music to his ears. The property was teeming with life, from towering pine trees to scampering squirrels, and every inch of it was a testament to Alan's vision of an oasis of peace.

One evening, as the sun set painting the sky in hues of orange and pink, Alan led Chantal to the house. The serenity of the place, combined with the underlying tension of their mission, created a unique atmosphere. As they walked hand in hand, the rustle of leaves beneath their feet felt therapeutic. "I built this with you in mind," Alan whispered, his eyes searching Chantal's for a response. The soft glow of the setting sun illuminated her face as she looked around, taking in the beauty of their surroundings. They both realized that, in these trying times, this sanctuary would serve a dual purpose: a place of strategic planning for the society and a testament to a dream they shared. This safe house would play a pivotal role in the days to come, a stronghold where strategies were devised, plans laid out, and dreams nurtured.

Chapter 11

Heartbeats

The weight of the recent events had led Alan to a moment of introspection. Sitting by the window, he allowed his mind to drift back to the days of their youth. Alan and Chantal, as fate would have it, had known each other their whole lives. Their families were close, their homes just a few blocks apart, and childhood photos often featured the two of them in the backdrop, sharing a playground or a birthday cake. There was an invisible string that always tied them together, a connection that was palpable to those around them. Yet, it took 35 years for that bond to transcend into something more profound. The memory of that transformation was crystal clear in Alan's mind: they were headed to a family party, the air thick with anticipation and unspoken sentiments. As they walked, side by side, the tension grew until Alan, in a rare moment of impulsiveness, pulled Chantal close and kissed her. That one act changed the course of their relationship, turning their deep-rooted friendship into a passionate love affair.

Chantal's diary served as a reservoir of their shared moments. She often recalled how Alan's spontaneous and headstrong nature contrasted with her calm and stabilizing presence. "Alan is like a tempest," she had once written, "wild and unpredictable. Yet, amidst his storms, it's my voice, my touch, that brings him ashore." Alan, with his dreams that reached the stars, often found himself lost in the vast expanse of his ambitions. It was Chantal who would pull him back, grounding him with her wisdom and patience. She remembered the nights when his frustrations would threaten to consume him and how a simple conversation with her would illuminate his path.

Over the pages, Chantal described their symbiotic relationship. "We're like two pieces of a puzzle," she penned, "Alan with his wild dreams, and me, offering the roots to his wings." Their bond was a dance of fire and water, each element balancing the other. Alan's fervor found its match in Chantal's unwavering strength. His penchant for chasing the horizon was tempered by her innate ability to bring him back from the edge. She was his anchor, and he, her North Star. Together, they navigated the complexities of life, their love serving as both compass and guide.

The quiet town of Saint Jerome twinkled under a velvet canopy of stars. Its serenity contrasted with the turmoil brewing in Alan's heart. He found himself on Chantal's quaint balcony, which was adorned with cascading green plants and delicate fairy lights. The setting exuded a sense of intimacy. Chantal's home, an old Victorian structure, had this balcony jutting out, providing a perfect view of the town below and the vast sky above. Gentle night breezes carried the soft melodies of crickets, creating a serene ambiance. They sat close, their fingers entwined, a silent promise of togetherness hanging in the air. The town's quietness, coupled with the ambient sounds of nature, provided a backdrop that felt almost ethereal. A bottle of water stood between them, its contents occasionally poured into glasses that reflected the luminosity of the stars.

Alan took a deep breath, knowing this was the moment he had to be most vulnerable. He looked into Chantal's eyes, sensing her patient anticipation. "Chantal," he began, his voice cracking, "there's so much more to GlobeTrotter, to this mission, than I've let on." He detailed the stakes, the looming shadows of adversaries, the weight of carrying the dreams of so many, and the toll it took on his mind and soul. As he spoke, his voice fluctuated between determination, fear, and raw emotion. It wasn't just about the technological marvel he was creating; it was about reshaping society, standing against oppression, and facing very powerful enemies. This mission had consumed him, made him question his sanity at times, but he couldn't, wouldn't, back down.

Chantal, listening intently, could feel the immense burden Alan bore. Her eyes softened with compassion, and she squeezed his hand, signaling her unwavering presence. "Alan," she whispered, brushing a stray lock of hair from his forehead, "I've known you my whole life. I've seen you rise, fall, and rise again. This mission, it's vast, it's challenging, but it's noble. And I believe in it because I believe in you." She paused, letting her words sink in before continuing, "This journey won't be easy, but know this: you won't walk it alone. I'm here, with you, every step of the way." Her conviction, her faith in him, filled the space between them, fortifying their bond even more, if that was possible. In that moment, under the watchful gaze of the stars, two souls came together, united in purpose and love.

The old family home was an emblem of nostalgia, walls echoing memories of laughter, love, and life. The aged, mahogany wooden floors creaked beneath Alan's footsteps, each step evoking another fond memory from his childhood. Alan's mother sat in her favored armchair beside the window, her fingers working deftly on her latest puzzle on her tablet. The soft yellow light from the reading lamp illuminated the fine wrinkles on her face, each one telling its own tale. She looked up, her eyes—vibrant, and not clouded with age—shining with unmistakable pride and concern as she watched her oldest son. Alan kneeled beside her, taking her hand into his. "Mom," he whispered, knowing she was well aware of the storm he was stepping into. They shared a quiet moment, their bond evident in the unsaid words. "Alan," she finally said, her voice soft yet firm, "From the day you were born, I knew you were destined for greatness. But remember, with greatness comes responsibility, and danger." Her eyes grew distant, filled with memories of her son's stubborn childhood days, where once he set his heart on something, there was no turning back. She sighed, "I always knew that when you set your mind on a path, not even the fiercest storm could deter you."

In a different part of the house, the sounds of youthful laughter and banter filled the air. David and Nathaniel, Alan's two sons, sat engaged in a game of chess. The intricacies of the game reflect their complex relationship with their father's choices. David, the older of the two, had a calm and contemplative demeanor. Nathaniel, on the other hand, was more expressive, wearing his emotions on his sleeve. The room grew quiet as David made a strategic move, locking eyes with Nathaniel. "You know," he began, his voice thoughtful, "Dad's always been a force to reckon with. Just like in this game, he's always three steps ahead." Nathaniel smirked, retorting, "Oh, definitely. I mean, the government must be quaking in their boots with him on the other side." David paused, looking up with a grin, "Honestly, I wouldn't want to be the guy against him." They both chuckled, but underneath the light-hearted banter was a layer of apprehension. They were proud of their father, yet the magnitude of his endeavor wasn't lost on them.

One evening, as the sun dipped below the horizon, painting the sky in hues of gold and orange, Alan sat with his sons on the porch. The gentle hum of cicadas set the mood for a heart-to-heart. "Boys," Alan began, taking a deep breath, "I know my involvement in all of this isn't easy for you." David and Nathaniel exchanged glances, their protective instincts for their father evident. Nathaniel finally spoke up, "Dad, we worry. We see the weight you carry, the potential dangers. It's hard not to." Alan nodded, understanding their concerns. David, ever the thoughtful one, added, "But we also see the change you're bringing, the hope you're instilling. It's a legacy, Dad." The three shared a silent moment, the depth of their bond, their pride, their concerns, all palpable in the twilight.

Inside the dimly lit, spacious hall of the Society's main gathering space, members sat in a circle, creating an atmosphere of unity and trust. The wooden beams overhead cast elongated shadows as candles flickered in the center, casting a warm, golden glow. As one member started sharing, a pattern emerged. Cynthia, a middle-aged librarian with a sharp intellect, recounted her journey of discovering the truth about the government's secret operations. Tears glistened in her eyes as she spoke of the personal sacrifices she had to make for the greater good. Next, a young man named Raj, an immigrant who had faced discrimination and injustice since his arrival in Canada, conveyed the sense of belonging and acceptance he felt with the Society. As each member shared their narrative, vulnerabilities were laid bare, and a tapestry of struggles, resilience, and hope was woven. The room became an echo chamber of support, empathy, and mutual understanding, reaffirming the belief that they weren't just allies in a cause but a family bound by shared values and aspirations.

The importance of trust within the group couldn't be overemphasized, and personal bonds were the backbone of that trust. It was the middle of October, and the Society's members had discovered it was Alan's birthday soon. The next week, little did he know that as he walked into the main hall, a beautiful surprise awaited him. The once solemn room was now filled with vibrant colors, the sound of soft music, and an aroma of delicious food. Strings of fairy lights were strewn across, and a banner reading "Happy Birthday, Alan!" hung prominently at the center. Alan was taken aback, his usually composed face breaking into a broad smile of genuine surprise. The joy was evident, not just because of the celebration, but due to the realization of the deep connections he had fostered.

As the evening progressed, the Society's members took turns expressing their gratitude and admiration for Alan. Stories of his compassion, his unwavering commitment to the cause, and personal anecdotes of his kindness were shared. Laughter and cheerful banter filled the room, punctuated occasionally by moments of deep emotion. Chantal raised a toast, her voice trembling slightly with emotion, "To Alan, our beacon of hope. We are not just united by a cause; we are bound by love, trust, and mutual respect. Happy Birthday!" The clinking of glasses resonated through the room. Alan, visibly moved, addressed the gathering, "This isn't just my birthday; it's a celebration of our unity, our strength, and our resolve. Thank you for being more than just comrades. You are my family." The evening was a testament to the depth of personal relationships Alan had built within the Society, turning a group of like-minded individuals into a tight-knit family.

Chapter 12

Public Outcry

Across major cities in Canada, from Vancouver's bustling streets to Toronto's historic landmarks, spontaneous rallies sprouted, each radiating an energy that was both infectious and palpable. Having been inspired by the Society's message, citizens took it upon themselves to reach out to the organization, seeking guidance on how to echo their sentiments effectively. While these events were grassroots in nature, they bore the mark of the Society's influence. Some media outlets, especially independent journalists and smaller local channels that were not financed by the government, sensed the significance of these movements and provided coverage. Reporters on the ground captured earnest testimonials of citizens, recounting stories of injustice and underscoring the urgency of the Society's mission. The media, particularly those brave enough to defy government narratives, played a pivotal role in amplifying the people's voice, making it impossible for the broader public to ignore the groundswell of sentiment.

The streets were alive with a colorful tapestry of peaceful protests. Artists painted murals that depicted hopeful visions of a brighter future, while others erected installations that critiqued the current regime's oppressive tactics. Musicians, poets, and performers took to makeshift stages, their art reflecting the Society's goals, entwining both melody and message to enthrall passersby. Children with painted faces roamed the crowds, their innocence juxtaposed against the weight of the cause. Everywhere one looked, there was a sense of unity in diversity, a collective consciousness that resonated with the desire for change. However, as with any large-scale movement, there were elements seeking to disrupt the harmony. As Alan had anticipated, the government planted rogue protesters amidst genuine participants. Their goal was simple: to create chaos and taint the

Society's reputation. These agents provocateurs attempted to incite violence, hurling stones, or shouting inflammatory slogans.

But Alan, with his astute foresight, had been several steps ahead. Recognizing a pattern he had observed in recent years, where genuine protests were sabotaged by government-instigated violence, he had prepared in advance. At each rally, special security teams, comprising individuals trained to handle disruptions peacefully, were embedded within the crowds. Their primary mission was to identify potential troublemakers and neutralize any situation before it escalated. With a mix of de-escalation techniques and quick intervention, these teams ensured that the true spirit of the rallies remained untainted. They worked discreetly, almost like shadows, ensuring that the focus remained on the people's voice, not the provocations. Alan's vigilance in anticipating this government tactic not only protected the protesters but also reinforced the public's faith in the Society's commitment to peaceful change.

Within the heart of a dimly lit studio, a spotlight shone brightly on Alan and a few prominent members of the coalition. Seated across them were journalists known for their integrity and commitment to the truth. These journalists, often operating outside the dominant narrative, took it upon themselves to shed light on the stories that truly mattered. As the interviews began, the camera captured the sincere expressions of Alan and his peers, their every word laden with conviction. They discussed their motives, detailed their plans, and underscored the urgency of the situation. Questions were probing but fair, and answers were candid, reflecting the deep commitment each member held for the cause. The interviews, though meant for national broadcast, were initially met with resistance. Traditional broadcasting avenues either refused to air them or were forced to cut them short. However, the digital age had its own power. These discussions found their way onto various social media platforms, from Twitter threads to Instagram stories, and even video clips on YouTube. As they were shared, commented upon, and re-shared, their reach became unstoppable. Like a prairie fire fueled by the wind, the message spread far and wide, reaching even those corners of the country previously untouched by the Society's influence.

On the other side of the spectrum, the government-backed media machinery swung into action, painting a starkly different picture. Newsrooms, well-funded and supported by the state, began their broadcasts with carefully curated images and clips, aiming to show the Society and its supporters in a negative light. Cleverly edited videos, selective quotes taken out of context, and flashy headlines accused Alan and his coalition of being disruptive, chaotic, and even dangerous. These broadcasts appealed to a certain section of the populace - the ones who never questioned the status quo, who took their daily news at face value, never probing deeper. The ones often referred to as the "usual sheep." For them, this narrative was gospel, and they remained convinced of the Society's so-called "nefarious" intentions.

However, the wider public, having been disillusioned by years of misleading narratives, recognized these tactics for what they were: propaganda. They had come to understand that the mainstream media, with its vested interests and agendas, could no longer be wholly trusted. Whispers in coffee shops, debates in public squares, and discussions around dinner tables echoed the same sentiment: the mainstream media had lost its credibility. Instead, people began to rely on independent journalists, influencers who upheld the truth, and, most importantly, their own discerning judgment. The trust once placed in large media houses had now shifted to smaller, independent voices who dared to speak the truth. And in this battle of narratives, while the mainstream tried to muddy the waters, the truth, as represented by Alan and his coalition, shimmered through, its clarity unmistakable.

The capital city of Ottawa, usually composed and dignified, was undergoing a significant transformation. Every available space—parks, streets, and public squares—seemed to have been claimed by people. Tents dotted the landscape as makeshift accommodations for those who had traveled far. Local businesses, cafes, and eateries saw an unprecedented surge in patrons, as people from the furthest corners of Canada converged upon Ottawa. Banners with supportive slogans swayed in the wind, children sporting face paint ran about excitedly, while elders sat on benches discussing the change they hoped to witness in their lifetimes. The crowd was a testament to the inclusivity of the movement. There were blue-collar workers standing shoulder to shoulder with white-collar professionals. Students and teachers, parents and grandparents, everyone irrespective of their age, race, or political beliefs, had gathered under the collective banner of change.

As the sun began to dip, casting a golden hue over Parliament Hill, the main stage of the rally came alive. One by one, coalition members took to the podium, their speeches echoing through the vast space. They recounted stories of struggles and triumphs, personal anecdotes of how the Society had changed their lives, and visions of a brighter future for Canada. Each speaker, in their unique way, managed to touch a chord with the audience. Moments of laughter were punctuated with instances of profound reflection. Yet, there was an unmistakable undercurrent of anticipation in the air. Everyone awaited the moment when Alan would step onto the stage. And when he did, the crowd erupted in deafening cheers.

Alan's address, unlike any other, was charged with an unparalleled intensity. His voice, seasoned by years of struggle and determination, carried with it the weight of responsibility and hope. He spoke of the humble beginnings of the Society, how a small group's desire for change had now snowballed into a national movement. He recalled the challenges they had faced, the sacrifices made, and the victories, however small, that had kept them going. But beyond reminiscing about the past, Alan painted a vivid picture of the future—a Canada where every citizen was given their due, where fairness and justice weren't just lofty ideals but lived realities. By the end of his speech, many in the crowd were moved to tears, while others took up a spontaneous chant, echoing their unwavering support for the cause. The rally in Ottawa was more than just an event; it was a historic juncture, signaling the dawn of a new era for the nation.

The grandeur of the Prime Minister's office was betrayed by the palpable tension that filled the air. Plush leather chairs, exquisite art pieces, and gold-accented furnishings all appeared inconsequential in the face of the mammoth screen which dominated the room. On it, the enormous crowd at Ottawa broadcasted their defiance and support for the coalition's cause. As the camera panned across to showcase Alan speaking fervently, capturing the rapt attention of every person present at the rally, a collective sigh resonated through the room. Close aides and advisors shifted uneasily, sharing worried glances. It was clear the government had underestimated the power of a united populace.

Prime Minister Trudeau's usually composed demeanor was nowhere to be seen. His face was a shade of crimson, the veins on his temple bulging visibly. With every applause and cheer from the rally, his grip on the armrest tightened. Cabinet members, huddled around him, whispered hurriedly, trying to come up with strategies and countermeasures. Some tried to console Trudeau, reassuring him that this was just a temporary surge and would wane with time. But deep down, they all knew that the magnitude of this rally, this public expression of discontent, was unlike anything they had encountered before even compared to the truckers rally a few years prior. A small flicker of doubt began to ignite in their minds. Was their leadership genuinely in jeopardy?

In the following days, covert meetings were held at undisclosed locations. High profile business tycoons, media barons, and influential policymakers were summoned, each one potentially holding the power to tilt public sentiment. Trudeau, in hushed conversations, promised them incentives—lucrative contracts, tax breaks, and monetary grants. However, these moguls, with their finger on the pulse of the nation, could sense the shifting tides. They had seen leaders rise and fall, and they knew when to hedge their bets. Many remained non-committal, giving vague assurances but refraining from promising outright support. They could see a future where Trudeau wasn't at the helm, and in the intricate game of power and politics, they weren't willing to back the losing horse. As Trudeau and his cabinet tried to rally their once steadfast allies, they found themselves increasingly isolated, a testament to the coalition's growing might.

Chapter 13

Cornered Wolves

The mahogany table that occupied the center of the room had been witness to many high-stakes conversations, but none like the one that transpired that evening. As Trudeau and his cabinet convened in the dimly lit room, a hush of nervous anticipation settled. Trudeau, looking visibly agitated, placed a file with a red classified stamp on the table. Inside were detailed profiles of the Society's prominent members. With a determined look, he suggested invoking the terrorism laws to freeze their assets. "It's the quickest way to cripple them," he argued, fingers tapping impatiently on the file.

However, an advisor, looking uneasy, chimed in, "Prime Minister, I don't believe that's advisable. Remember the truckers' incident? We tried a similar tactic, and it backfired horribly. The courts won't be on our side this time." Murmurs of agreement resonated through the room. The truckers fiasco was a glaring example of a strategy that not only failed but also turned public sentiment fiercely against the administration. That misstep had cost them dearly, and no one wanted a repeat of it.

But as the weight of the situation bore down on them, the cohesion of Trudeau's once unified cabinet started to splinter. A clear divide began to manifest. One faction, recognizing the burgeoning strength of the Society, believed the time was ripe for negotiations. "We can't keep opposing them. Maybe we should consider a middle ground, some sort of dialogue," a member suggested. On the other end, hardliners in the cabinet were not ready to capitulate. They urged aggressive actions, even if covert, to stifle Alan and the coalition's momentum. "A show of strength is what's needed," one declared, "we have to nip this in the bud before it gets any bigger!" However, even they were aware of the inherent risks. An aggressive stance could potentially galvanize more support for the Society, turning them into martyrs. As the hours wore on, disagreements flared, voices were raised, and Trudeau, once again in his leadership, found himself at a crossroads, unsure of which path to tread.

Amidst the political turmoil and public support for the Society, the government made a desperate attempt to regain control of the narrative. In an official press release, they labeled the Society as potential agitators, subtly implying the possible imposition of punitive measures against them. However, this attempt to smear the Society's reputation landed flat. Journalists, even from mainstream media who were traditionally more government-friendly, buried the story in the inner pages or gave it scant coverage in television segments. It was a testament to how far the tide of public opinion had shifted against Trudeau and his administration.

The next morning, the government's statement became a laughingstock online. Social media was awash with memes poking fun at Trudeau's desperate attempts to tarnish the coalition. One particularly popular meme depicted Trudeau as a frustrated kindergarten teacher, trying to discipline a class full of mischievous students with the caption, "Class, stop supporting the Society or you'll get detention!" Another meme had Trudeau's face superimposed on a scene from the film 'Titanic,' with the ship labeled 'Government' hitting the iceberg labeled 'The Society.' The caption read, "It's just a small fringe minority. What could go wrong?" The digital space echoed with laughter and mockery, further undermining the government's standing.

In the midst of this online merriment, Alan's day took a darker turn. A shadowy figure, clearly a covert operative, discreetly approached him while he was at a café. With a cold and calculated demeanor, the man delivered a thinly veiled threat, suggesting severe consequences if Alan persisted with his movement. However, Alan, unshaken and undeterred, stared the man down. The café's ambient noise seemed to fade as the two locked eyes. After a tense moment, Alan responded, "You can go back and tell Trudeau that his time is nearly up." Pausing for effect and with a smirk, Alan added, "And let him know he should start packing for his forced retirement." The operative, taken aback by Alan's audacity, retreated without another word.

With the increasing tension and political underhandedness, those closest to Alan became unsuspecting targets. It began subtly at first. His mother and sons started noticing unmarked vehicles parked near their homes and strangers asking questions about their connections to Alan. But it soon escalated. One evening, a pair of local authorities paid a visit to the home of David where Nathaniel happened to be, Alan's sons. Claiming it was a routine inquiry, their line of questioning was clearly aimed at pressuring the young men to use their influence over their father. However, David and Nathaniel were their father's sons. With defiant glares, Nathaniel questioned, "Do you even enjoy your job? Because I doubt you'll have it for long after my dad learns about this little 'visit'." David, with equal grit, chimed in, "Seems like you're picking the wrong side of history here." The officers, feeling outnumbered and outmaneuvered, beat a hasty retreat. Lise, Alan's mother, also got a visit but what they hadn't realized was that Lise, was more than just a mother and grandmother. She was an acclaimed author, with a dedicated following that numbered in the millions. They loved her for her insight, her depth, and her ability to connect with readers on a personal level. These loyal fans wouldn't take kindly to authorities harassing their beloved author's family.

The government's attempts to deter Alan's inner circle didn't end with his immediate family. On a clear afternoon, as Chantal was leaving her office, she was approached by a face from her past. François, a former friend and now a mid-level government bureaucrat, tried to play on their history. "Chantal," he began, his voice drenched in faux concern, "You need to distance yourself from Alan. It's not safe." He hinted at the possibility of dire consequences for those who continued to associate with the leader of the Society. But Chantal, empowered by her love for Alan and her conviction in the cause, merely laughed. "François," she said with a hint of pity, "It's not me who needs to be rethinking their associations. If I were you, I'd start looking for a new job. Because once

Trudeau's reign crumbles, and trust me it will, you'll find yourself out in the cold." François, taken aback by her boldness, could only muster a flustered look before slinking away, realizing that threats would have no effect on this determined woman.

In the dimly lit room, echoing with hushed murmurs, the members of the Society gathered, sensing the gravity of the situation. Alan, with a demeanor that radiated both determination and reassurance, stepped forward. His voice, always measured and controlled, conveyed a blend of caution and optimism. "Friends," he began, "The time has come for us to acknowledge the real pressures we face. There have been threats, attempts at intimidation, and unsavory tactics targeting our loved ones." He paused, his gaze meeting each of theirs in turn. "But know this," he continued, "They wouldn't be so desperate if we weren't making an impact. I want each of you to understand that I am not bowing to these threats. I have contingencies in place, and I am prepared for the long fight ahead." Alan's words served as a rallying cry, a testament to his unyielding spirit. He emphasized that while the path ahead was fraught with challenges, they should trust in his leadership and in the righteousness of their cause.

As Alan's address came to an end, other members of the Society rose to share their stories. Jasmine, a young activist, described how her community center had been unexpectedly audited. Robert, a seasoned journalist, recounted receiving anonymous calls warning him to "stay away from the Society if he knew what was good for him." Each tale was a stitch in a tapestry of intimidation and coercion. Yet, instead of evoking fear, these stories galvanized the group. They became a united front, each narrative reinforcing their common purpose and the importance of their mission. The group, young and old, from all walks of life, began to see that the government's tactics were a testament to the Society's power and influence.

As the meeting drew to a close, the atmosphere in the room had shifted from initial apprehension to renewed commitment. "It's evident," remarked Eleanor, one of the senior members, "that this movement has grown beyond any single individual. It's not just about Alan or any of us; it's about the future of our nation and the ideals we hold dear." Nods of agreement and murmurs of affirmation echoed her sentiment. Everyone recognized that the Society's mission was now an unstoppable force, a tidal wave of change that would continue to grow, with or without any individual at its helm. The night concluded with a group pledge, a vow to persevere in the face of adversity and to uphold the vision they had all come together to realize.

Chapter 14

The Big Reveal

The bustling room, filled with buzzing computers and the occasional hum of servers, became the focal point of Alan's most ambitious project. Surrounded by an array of monitors, Alan meticulously refined the algorithms of his AI tool, an invention he believed would be the linchpin in exposing the web of government corruption. As he made final adjustments to the tool's parameters, he marveled at the scope of its capabilities. The AI, with all its agents, was designed to rapidly scan vast swathes of the internet, differentiating between the truth and the multitude of lies was, which government transaction was legal or not, and misinformation scattered across the digital realm. "We're on the cusp," he remarked to his team, "of revealing to the world an undeniable truth. We've aggregated more information than we could have manually done in a decade." The team huddled around one screen, collectively watching as lines of data streamed in. The sheer volume was staggering, but the AI tool had made it digestible, categorizing and prioritizing key pieces of evidence that were irrefutable.

However, as the date of the reveal approached, an air of tension permeated the Society's headquarters. During one of the routine meetings, a few members hesitantly voiced their anxieties. Miranda, a mother of two and an ardent supporter of the Society, spoke first. "I believe in what we're doing, Alan, but what if they come for us? For our families?" she questioned, her voice tinged with concern. Others murmured in agreement, reflecting a shared worry. Alan, pausing to take in the gravity of their fears, responded earnestly. "Every significant leap in history has always come with risks," he said, his voice echoing a deep-seated resolve. "But we have precautions in place." He then unveiled his safeguard mechanism: a failsafe that ensured the vast databank would instantly flood the internet should any harm come to him or any member of the Society. This digital deluge, he explained, would be too expansive and swift for any entity to contain, ensuring the truth reached the masses regardless of any attempt to suppress it. Alan said "The AI possesses an extensive databank, cataloging the indiscretions of every corrupt politician, judge, and individuals wielding power, leaving no stone unturned in its quest for truth."

The reassurance offered by this failsafe, coupled with Alan's unwavering dedication, bolstered the group's confidence. Samantha, one of the Society's tech experts, voiced a sentiment shared by many: "With this AI and the failsafe, it feels like we have an impenetrable shield. They can't stop the truth from emerging." Alan nodded in agreement, adding, "This isn't just about exposing lies, but about reigniting hope and trust in a system that has long betrayed its citizens." The meeting concluded with a renewed sense of purpose, each member invigorated by the impending revelation and the profound change it promised to bring.

As dawn broke, a video, bearing the emblem of the Society, surfaced across the vast expanse of social media platforms. It began with a panning shot of the serene Canadian landscape, symbolizing the pure essence of the nation. Then, Alan's familiar face appeared, confidence and gravity in his eyes. "Soon," he began, "the truths that have been buried deep will surface. Truths about those who have forgotten their duty to the people, and who have instead embraced corruption's tempting allure." As the video progressed, a silhouette representation of politicians, judges, and other powerful entities being exposed by beams of light illustrated the forthcoming revelations.

Word spread like wildfire. Everywhere, from coffee shops to office break rooms, Alan's teaser video was the talk of the town. Friends shared it, families discussed it, and debates arose about the possible revelations it promised. Would their local representative be implicated? What about the judge from the neighboring town? The video's potent mix of intrigue and promise had created an electric atmosphere across the country, leaving people eagerly awaiting what was to come. The suspense was palpable; for many, it felt like the eve of a major historical event.

News channels and online media outlets were on a frenzied spree. Every reporter and journalist wanted the scoop, to be the first to uncover and report the depth of the rot. Politicians, usually ready with their practiced statements and calculated responses, now found themselves cornered. Television screens were filled with images of journalists thrusting microphones at retreating politicians and influential individuals. When quizzed about their possible involvement or if they feared exposure, most evaded the question, faces flustered, simply responding with a terse, "No comment." But behind those two words lay a world of anxiety, doubt, and the dawning realization that their past actions might finally be catching up with them.

The clock struck the appointed hour, and viewers from across the nation, indeed, the world, tuned in, with bated breath, to the live-streamed event. It opened with the Society's emblem, followed by a hauntingly slow pan of the National Parliament Buildings—a symbol of promise that had turned into a bastion of secrets for many. As the view transitioned, Alan stood in a dimly lit room, with multiple screens behind him, ready to reveal the findings. "Tonight," Alan began, his voice calm yet firm, "we pull back the curtains on the machinations that have gnawed at the foundations of our democracy. With irrefutable evidence, we will shine a light on the shadows." Alan quickly explained a little about is artificial intelligence program with millions of "agents" (other ai's that each had a mission of finding data that reported back to the main ai to be sorted.

For the next few hours, a tsunami of information was unveiled. Alan, like a skilled maestro, conducted the presentation, meticulously showcasing the AI's findings. He began with the least influential individuals, slowly building the anticipation. Each revelation was backed by visual proofs: clips of under-the-table deals, images of documents showing illicit approvals, and digital records of hefty bank transfers, often to offshore accounts. The sheer scale of corruption was astonishing; no corner of the political or judiciary world seemed untouched. As each corrupt deed was laid bare, a real-time tally on the side of the screen kept track, painting a damning picture.

Yet, what gripped the viewers the most were the interviews. Whistleblowers, some anonymous with distorted voices, others bold enough to appear on camera, recounted their experiences, shared their stories of being strong-armed into unethical practices, and spoke of the threats they faced when they hesitated. The narrative that emerged was one of a deeply entrenched network of power players, operating with impunity and without any moral compass. This wasn't just a mere revelation; it was an indictment of a system that had gone astray. The nation watched, appalled and riveted, as the depth of the decay was laid bare before them.

The tremors of the revelations sent shockwaves across the digital realm. Within mere minutes of the stream ending, social media platforms were set ablaze with reactions. On Twitter, hashtags such as #BigReveal, #TruthAI, and #CorruptionExposed shot to the top, with millions sharing their thoughts, feelings, and overwhelming disbelief. While citizens expressed their anger, memes, infographics, and videos flooded timelines, simplifying the complex webs of deceit for the average person. Even platforms like TikTok and Instagram were filled with influencers and celebrities sharing their personal reactions, some even composing songs to capture the zeitgeist of the moment. Renowned international media houses, from BBC to Al Jazeera, CNN to NHK, picked up the story, making it a global sensation. Within 48 hours, the video's view count on YouTube surpassed iconic music videos and speeches, and with AI translators making it accessible in every conceivable language, the story was resonating in every corner of the world.

Government officials, especially those named and shamed in the findings, went into a frenzy. National TV channels and radio stations were filled with politicians attempting to salvage their reputations. Some, with a facade of bravado, tried to challenge the authenticity of the information, labeling it as doctored or taken out of context. They shouted about witch-hunts, painting themselves as victims of a grand conspiracy. Others chose to downplay their involvement, arguing that while they might have been involved in certain dealings, they had not directly benefited or were unaware of the illicit nature of the transactions. However, these voices were in the minority. A more considerable number of officials found themselves paralyzed by the undeniable evidence, opting for silence, hoping that the storm would pass. But for some, the weight of their actions and the public's disdain was too much. Resignation letters began pouring in, not just from low-level bureaucrats but also from some high-ranking officials, admitting their guilt, either implicitly or explicitly, and stepping down from their positions of power.

Yet, amid the chaos, the integrity of the AI tool was never in doubt. The meticulous methodology and the multi-layered checks ensured that every piece of information was accurate, turning skepticism into acceptance for most. The country, which had for so long been kept in the dark, was now navigating through a maze of truths, each more shocking than the last. The question on everyone's lips was, "What happens next?"

Chapter 15

Tides of Change

The sheer magnitude of the revelations had the entire nation reeling. In towns and cities stretching from Vancouver to Newfoundland, Canadians were coming to terms with the unveiled truths, which triggered a range of emotions, from fury and indignation to sorrow and disbelief. Protests, both planned and spontaneous, erupted across city squares and outside government buildings. In Vancouver, students from UBC and SFU marched in unison, chanting slogans and brandishing placards decrying the exposed corruption. Meanwhile, in Montreal's Place des Arts, artists used the medium of street art and performances to give voice to the collective anger. The Maritimes weren't left out either; town hall meetings became common, with community leaders facilitating open forums where citizens voiced their frustrations, shared their stories, and brainstormed on the way forward. What was initially a government scandal had transformed into a grassroots movement, and Canadians from all walks of life were connecting, sharing, and mobilizing on a scale never seen before.

Major media outlets, which had previously maintained a somewhat neutral stance, now found themselves thrust into the epicenter of the storm. The journalists, who had been silent spectators, were now pressed to take on a more assertive role. TV anchors and radio show hosts, known for their mellow and reserved nature, became persistent interrogators overnight. Nightly news programs were filled with interviews where implicated officials were asked hard-hitting questions. Panel discussions were dominated by talk of ethical accountability and the depth of rot within the system. With every official's stutter or evasion, public trust in the exposed members of the establishment further dwindled. Newsrooms were flooded with calls from Canadians demanding justice, and the media ensured these voices were amplified.

In the more formal corridors of power, the reactions were more structured but no less intense. The talk of resignations became a daily occurrence. Some politicians, with their careers and reputations irrevocably tarnished, saw resigning as the only viable option, hoping it might salvage a modicum of dignity. But mere resignations wouldn't suffice for many Canadians; they demanded accountability. There were growing calls for criminal investigations into the most egregious acts of corruption, with some even demanding jail time for the guilty. In the House of Commons, murmurs of a vote of "No Confidence" began to circulate, signaling a potential toppling of the government. The nation was on the precipice of monumental change, and it seemed the tides had turned irreversibly against the old guard.

Inside the ornate chambers of the Prime Minister's office, the atmosphere was thick with tension. Behind the closed doors of 24 Sussex Drive, top advisors and close confidants to Trudeau gathered in what many considered the most crucial meeting of his political tenure. The room was split. On one side, the pragmatists argued fervently for immediate damage control. "We need to go public, hold a press conference, show the people that we're still in control," one advisor asserted, "Even if it's just an acknowledgement of the situation and an assurance of internal investigations." Their belief was that with the right strategy, they could weather the storm, at least for a while. These were the individuals who had seen political careers resurrected from the ashes before and believed that with enough spin, they could turn the tide of public opinion.

But on the other side of the room were those who had lost all hope. Their faces were etched with exhaustion and defeat. "Justin," one of his oldest friends began, his voice heavy with emotion, "Maybe it's time. Maybe it's time to step down and let someone else take the reins." Their rationale was simple. With the breadth of allegations, denials would only go so far. Stepping down might be the only way to save face and leave with a shred of dignity intact. These were the voices of those who believed in Trudeau, not just the politician, but the man, and they thought his resignation might be the only way to salvage his legacy.

In the midst of these heated exchanges, Trudeau sat contemplatively, his usual charismatic demeanor replaced with a somberness that few had seen before. He looked out the window, seemingly lost in the weight of his thoughts. For him, this was more than just a political crisis; it was a personal reckoning. He reflected on his journey to leadership, the promises he had made to the Canadian people, and the choices that had brought him to this point. Memories of past victories, jubilant crowds, and landmark decisions flashed before him. Yet, in these reflections, there was a glaring absence of personal accountability. He mulled over strategies and decisions, looking for external factors, systemic issues, or unforeseen challenges to blame. While he grappled with the fallout, in his heart, he found it hard to admit any direct responsibility. This inability to internalize blame, a trait that had often served him well in the tumultuous world of politics, now isolated him further from his team and the nation he led.

In various corners of the country, from bustling urban centers to quaint town halls, Society members convened, their energy palpable. The weight of their revelations had shifted the national narrative and had given them an unprecedented platform. As they met, the focus was clear: strategize on harnessing this momentum to create lasting change. While many in the Society believed they had the government on the ropes, they were also acutely aware that political tides could change quickly. "We have a window of opportunity," one seasoned member commented, "and we need to act swiftly and smartly." Brainstorming sessions took place, with members suggesting community outreach initiatives, further investigations, and even the possibility of running for public offices. They recognized that while they had revealed the truth, the real challenge lay ahead in ensuring that this new era of transparency and accountability became the norm.

The global dimension of their movement began to crystalize as well. Word of the Society's crusade reached international shores, catching the attention of significant figures in the global arena. Among those who publicly lauded the Society's efforts were two Members of the European Parliament, known for their outspoken stance against corruption and their advocacy for transparent governance. Christine Anderson of Germany, with her signature eloquence, took to the floor of the parliament, praising the resilience and determination of the Society. She emphasized the universal values they upheld, stating, "The fight against corruption and for transparency is not just a Canadian fight; it's a global imperative." On the other hand, Mislav Kolakusic of Croatia, known for his fiery speeches and no-nonsense attitude, hailed the Society as a beacon of hope. During a televised interview, he passionately urged other nations to take a leaf out of the Society's book and usher in an era where those in power are always held accountable.

This international endorsement was not just a morale booster for the Society; it was a strategic boon. The backing of influential figures like Anderson and Kolakusic expanded the reach of their message, offering a layer of protection against any potential backlash and further isolating corrupt elements within the Canadian government. With such global support, the Society's mission transcended borders, becoming a symbol of a global movement for change, accountability, and transparency. They realized that their fight was no longer just about one nation's governance; it was about setting a precedent for democracies everywhere.

The Canadian government, once a global symbol of stability and order, now found itself in a state of flux. The revelations brought forth by the Society had shaken its very core, prompting several high-ranking officials and cabinet members to tender their resignations. The nation watched as familiar faces, once seen as untouchable figures of authority, stepped down one after the other. Their public statements were a mix of carefully worded apologies, expressions of regret, and justifications. However, to the discerning public, these resignations reflected more than just personal decisions; they were a testament to the undeniable power of truth and collective action.

Trudeau, the Prime Minister himself, could not remain silent amid this political maelstrom. The weight of expectation bore heavily on him as the nation waited with bated breath for his response. When he finally appeared on national television, the atmosphere was thick with anticipation. He stood against a backdrop of the iconic maple leaf flag, looking visibly subdued. Throughout his speech, he carefully threaded the line, addressing the revelations without admitting to any personal wrongdoing. He spoke of his love for Canada and its people, his commitment to the country, and the need for transparency and reform. While many criticized him for not directly admitting to the allegations, others noted the somber tone of his address, recognizing the gravity of the situation.

However, the most significant part of his speech came towards its conclusion. Trudeau, perhaps understanding the irreversible nature of the political landscape, announced his resignation as the Prime Minister of Canada. He emphasized the need for a fresh start and a government that truly embodied the ideals and aspirations of its people. His commitment to ensuring a peaceful transition of power was a clear sign that he recognized the changing tides. The nation stood still in that moment, absorbing the gravity of his words. This was not just the resignation of a Prime Minister but a significant turning point in Canada's political history. The events set in motion by the Society's revelations had culminated in a clear message: the people's voice, when united, could bring about change, even in the highest echelons of power.

Chapter 16

A New Dawn

Within the political upheaval and resignations, Canada found itself at a crossroads, with the daunting task of reconstructing a government that had lost the trust of its citizens. The need for a new, interim government was paramount, and there was an undeniable sense of urgency. Political analysts, intellectuals, and leaders of various communities were summoned to brainstorm the structure and guidelines for this nascent entity. Roundtable discussions were held nationwide, with citizens actively voicing their expectations and demands. The common consensus centered on three core principles: reforms, unprecedented transparency, and increased public participation in governance. The country had tasted the bitterness of deceit and corruption and was now resolute in its demand for a trustworthy, transparent administration.

In light of the Society's instrumental role in unveiling the truth and catalyzing change, their involvement in the restoration process was seen as essential. News broke out that Alan's Society had been approached to play an active role in the transition team. This decision was met with widespread approval, as the public saw the Society as a beacon of hope and a guarantor of transparency. Alan, being the spearhead of the Society, was offered a specific role in overseeing the integration of the GlobeTrotter Ecosystem into the Canadian administrative framework. The GlobeTrotter Ecosystem, revered for its potential in promoting transparency, was deemed a critical tool for the nation's rejuvenation. Alan accepted this responsibility, recognizing its pivotal role in restoring public faith.

However, the Society's primary goal remained unaltered. While individual members like Alan took on specialized roles in the transition, the Society at large reaffirmed its commitment to remain a vigilant overseer of the entire process. They formally announced their decision to function as watchdogs, ensuring the principles of transparency and accountability were upheld without compromise until the GlobeTrotter Ecosystem was up and working. With a nationwide network and the unwavering support of the masses, they pledged to keep a hawk's eye on every decision, policy, and action of the interim government. Their message was clear: while they were partners in the process of nation-building, they would never shy away from calling out any deviations from the path of righteousness.

The cobblestone streets of Old Quebec were drenched in history and every brick whispered tales of the past. The city, with its centuries-old architecture and the gentle flow of the Saint Lawrence River, offered a serene backdrop for introspection. Alan found himself wandering through these streets, soaking in the ambiance and the weight of the moment. Each step he took resonated with the footprints of his tumultuous journey – from the inception of an idea, a mere spark, to the blazing fire of a movement that had transformed an entire nation. He passed by cafes, where patrons would nod in recognition or raise their glasses to him, and musicians played tunes that hinted at change and hope.

However, as he walked, Alan's thoughts were not solely of triumph. They were punctuated by memories of the many sleepless nights, the strategic meetings that stretched into the wee hours, the threats and intimidation, and the countless times he had questioned the path he had chosen. He recalled the faces of doubters, naysayers who had dismissed his endeavors as fleeting and inconsequential. But among these challenging memories were also recollections of victories, however small. Each time the Society made a breakthrough, every moment the public rallied behind them, and the joy of seeing corrupt officials being held accountable for their actions. These were the sparks that kept the fire burning, constantly reminding Alan and his team of the bigger picture.

At the heart of these reflections, however, was a deep-seated understanding of the importance of conviction. As the sun began to set, casting the old city in a golden hue, Alan found himself standing by the river's edge. The flowing waters seemed symbolic of time, reminding him of the transient nature of life. It brought forth a realization of how crucial it was to stand up for one's beliefs, no matter the odds. For if not now, then when? And if not him, then who? The ripples in the water, much like the ripples of his movement, signified that even a single stone could create waves. Alan's heart swelled with a mix of pride, humility, and an undying resolve to continue the fight for justice, truth, and transparency.

The venue was a sprawling tech park in Toronto, a symbol of modernity juxtaposed against a city rich in history. Skyscrapers towered in the background, but the focus of all was the enormous, futuristic dome at the center, with the words "GlobeTrotter Ecosystem: The Dawn of a New Era" illuminated in gleaming neon. The anticipation was palpable as people from all walks of life poured into the area. The grandeur of the event was not lost on anyone. Esteemed tech gurus arrived, discussing the potential of the new ecosystem with fervor. Environmentalists could be seen nodding approvingly at the various green technologies that were incorporated. Politicians, usually divided in their stances, for once stood united in their admiration and hope for this new endeavor. The public, armed with cameras and smartphones, captured every moment, eager to be part of history.

When the time came for the official unveiling, a hush fell upon the crowd. The dome's lights dimmed, replaced by an intricate light show that told the story of the GlobeTrotter Ecosystem's inception. From Alan's early blueprints and the tireless work of engineers to the challenges and breakthroughs, it was a visual journey that captivated all in attendance. As the narrative progressed, key features of the ecosystem were highlighted — its innovative technologies, its dedication to sustainable and green solutions, and its potential to revolutionize not only Canada but potentially the world. As the light show concluded, panels of the wall retracted to unveil the series of supercomputers, the functional prototype of the GlobeTrotter Ecosystem. There it stood, a beacon of innovation, with terminals demonstrating real-time data collection, security, and AI-driven tools to foster transparency and accountability.

The aftermath of the presentation was a flurry of discussions, demonstrations, and accolades. Major tech websites and news outlets hailed the GlobeTrotter Ecosystem as the epitome of innovation for the modern age. Environmentalists praised its focus on sustainability and its potential to drastically reduce the inequalities people had suffered so far. Politicians saw it as a testament to Canada's renewed dedication to progress and transparency. At the heart of all these discussions was the overarching sentiment that the GlobeTrotter Ecosystem was not merely a technological marvel; it was the embodiment of the new Canadian spirit. A spirit that was innovative, leaving no one behind, and constantly looking ahead to a brighter future. It was a reflection of a country that had learned from its past and was eager to forge a path forward, setting an example for the world to follow.

In the wake of the launch of the GlobeTrotter Ecosystem, the most immediate and significant change Canadians experienced in this first leg was the implementation of Universal Basic Income (UBI). Every citizen above the age of 16, regardless of employment status or background, began receiving a stipend. This financial cushion drastically transformed the socioeconomic landscape. Families who had previously been burdened by debt or living hand-to-mouth found relief. Young adults and students were provided the freedom to pursue further education or entrepreneurial ventures without the looming pressure of financial instability. Many observers commented on the uplifting aura that seemed to envelope cities and towns, as a collective weight had been lifted off the shoulders of millions.

Alongside the implementation of UBI, Canadians witnessed a profound transformation in their tax structure. Sales taxes, often criticized as regressive, were completely abolished for everyday essentials, making basic goods more affordable for the masses. While this was the case, luxury items maintained their tax component, ensuring that those with the means to procure opulent items continued to equitably contribute to the state's finances. Simultaneously, the longstanding personal income tax was entirely eradicated, empowering individuals to keep a larger chunk of their hard-earned money. This fueled increased consumer spending and investment. To counterbalance this, an innovative "hoarding tax" was introduced, where individuals holding over 1 million Globies in their digital wallets were subjected to a 10% taxation, discouraging the extreme accumulation of wealth.

Moreover, businesses were now automatically taxed 30% on their sales, with two-thirds of this amount channeled directly into bolstering the UBI system, and the remaining third aiding governmental functions. This novel approach not only ensured a consistent inflow to support UBI but also guaranteed a robust revenue for the government. Furthermore, thanks to the ingenious design of the GlobeTrotter Ecosystem, tax evasion became a relic of the past. The transparent and incorruptible nature of this digital framework meant that every transaction was accounted for, ensuring that resources were used to their utmost potential and that every cent was accounted for. The seamless integration of these measures ushered in an era of fairness, transparency, and efficiency.

The impact on the Canadian job market was significant. With streamlined and more efficient government systems, bureaucracy was significantly reduced, enabling quicker decision-making processes. As a result, unemployment rates plummeted. The economic terrain became fertile ground for startups and innovative ventures. With UBI serving as a safety net, many Canadians took the leap into entrepreneurship, resulting in a flourish of new small businesses across sectors. The mining industry saw a resurgence of national pride as permits for foreign entities were revoked, ensuring that Canada's rich natural resources benefited its own people first and foremost. The energy sector underwent a revival, adopting more sustainable practices, yet seeing immense growth and profitability. Simultaneously, the introduction of the Globie, along with its associated tokens, became the bedrock of the new financial system, marking

Canada's bold step into a digital economic future. Perhaps most revolutionary was the shift in power dynamics. People now had a direct say in fiscal matters, casting votes on government spending and holding officials accountable. To top it all off, a revamped immigration policy ensured that while Canada remained open and inclusive, it did so in a manner that best served its national interests. It was a new dawn indeed.

As Alan sat down for his online session, there was a palpable tension in the virtual space. Screens from all over the country flickered with his face, and households tuned in to their televisions, awaiting his address about the second phase of the GlobeTrotter Ecosystem. He started gently, understanding the emotional and historical attachment people have to land ownership. "Ownership," he began, "is a human-made concept, and while it provides security and pride, it also creates division and inequalities." Alan elaborated on the paradox of land ownership, questioning the very premise of owning a slice of the Earth, a planet that existed millions of years before humans and would continue to do so long after. He painted a picture of a world where everyone had an equal stake and could live anywhere without the burden of astronomical property prices or the fear of eviction.

Expanding on the radical idea, Alan went on to elucidate how this new system would work in practice. "Imagine a Canada where every citizen has access to land, not based on their wealth or status but on their need and choice." He described a system where people would rent plots of land under conditions that granted them virtually all the rights that traditional ownership would. Whether it was for farming, building homes, or setting up businesses, the land would serve its tenant's purpose. This rental model would make land accessible to young couples looking to build their first homes, to indigenous communities looking to reclaim their ancestral territories, and to every Canadian in between. The egalitarian nature of this approach aimed to bridge the gap between the haves and the have-nots, making the dream of having one's own space a reality for many who had previously been priced out of the market.

But, the most innovative aspect of this plan lay in the reinvestment strategy. Alan, with a twinkle in his eye, declared, "Every cent generated from these land rentals will be funneled directly back into the UBI system." This meant that the very earth Canadians walked on would be contributing to their well-being, ensuring a more prosperous life for everyone. He assured that while the land might be rented, everything built upon it - every brick laid, every plant sowed, every business established - belonged unequivocally to the individual. Should they wish to relocate or sell their constructed assets, they could do so freely and then transfer their land rental agreement. Alan ended his session with a plea for trust and unity. He asked Canadians to reimagine a country where the land truly belonged to everyone, fostering a community where each individual had an equal stake in its vast and beautiful expanse.

With the success of the previous phases, the third leg of the GlobeTrotter Ecosystem brought about transformative changes in many foundational systems of society.

The stock markets, once driven purely by profit, underwent a renaissance. Their new design was grounded in sustainable growth and ethical investments. Companies listed were required to meet specific social, and governance criteria. This change ensured that investments were not only profitable but also beneficial to society. The educational system also experienced a rehaul. Traditional rote learning was phased out, making way for critical thinking, emotional intelligence, and hands-on experiential learning. Students were now prepared not just for jobs but to be well-rounded individuals, capable of navigating a rapidly changing world. Other industries like food and beverage and manufacturing shifted towards sustainable and local sourcing, ethical production practices, and a focus on quality over quantity. Services became more personalized and tailored to individual needs, healthcare became more preventive than curative, and transportation saw an influx of efficient means. Notably, the mental health industry saw significant investments and became accessible to everyone, ensuring the well-being of all citizens. Lastly, the legal system, which had historically been slow and tedious, adopted technology and transparency measures that made justice swift and fair.

The introduction of systems like cultural preservation ensured that indigenous communities and their histories were preserved and celebrated. Digital privacy became a fundamental right, with stringent laws in place to prevent unauthorized data access. But perhaps the most significant change was in the realm of artificial intelligence. With AI playing a significant role in the GlobeTrotter Ecosystem and in the future, new ethical standards were set. These standards ensured AI acted in the best interests of humanity, respecting individual rights, and always having transparent decision-making processes.

The formation of the new Justice Force marked a radical change in public security. It wasn't just a rebranding of the police force but a reimagining of the role of law enforcement in society. Their primary mission was to serve and protect the community while upholding the newly established ethical and societal standards. Rigorous training programs were developed, focusing not just on physical prowess but emotional intelligence, conflict resolution, and community engagement. The bar was set high, and as a result, many existing officers found it challenging to meet these new standards. Those who made the cut were individuals who exemplified the qualities of empathy, integrity, and dedication. They weren't just enforcers of the law; they were community builders, peacekeepers, and above all, they were accountable to the very people they served.

Epilogue

In the wake of the GlobeTrotter Ecosystem's implementation, Canada saw an unprecedented era of unity and strength. The vast expanses of the nation, from the rugged coasts of Newfoundland to the pristine landscapes of British Columbia, echoed with a singular voice of hope and optimism. Communities previously divided by political beliefs or economic disparities found common ground in the new system. Public spaces and digital platforms buzzed with stories of individuals who had experienced tangible improvements in their quality of life. People from diverse backgrounds were not only living side by side but thriving together. The spirit of collective welfare and inclusivity was palpable in the air. More and more people were beginning to believe that they lived in a nation that genuinely cared for their well-being.

Amidst this national rebirth, Alan and Chantal rediscovered each other. They found solace in shared memories, recounting their initial skeptical meetings, the ups and downs they had faced, and the countless nights they had spent strategizing and dreaming. Walking along the serene lakesides, they painted visions of a peaceful life off the grid, perhaps in a quaint cabin nestled in the Laurentians. Their bond, tested and strengthened by the trials they had undergone, now felt unbreakable. Chantal often joked about Alan's incessant persistence in the face of adversity, while Alan admired Chantal's unwavering belief in the good within people.

One sunny afternoon, Alan's family home was bustling with joy. Children ran around with laughter, the elderly shared stories of the past, and a palpable sense of gratitude filled the air. As the family sat around a large wooden table, laden with a sumptuous feast, Alan's mother raised a toast. She spoke of the pride she felt in her son's resilience and the hope he had instilled in millions. The gathering wasn't just a celebration of familial bonds but of dreams realized and a nation transformed. As night fell and the stars shone brightly overhead, the conversations shifted to the future. Whispers circulated about other countries keenly observing Canada's transformation. Citizens worldwide were rallying, demanding the same level of transparency, inclusivity, and prosperity that Canadians now enjoyed. The novel draws to a close with a vision of a world on the cusp of change, inspired by a nation that dared to dream and make those dreams a reality.

The real GlobeTrotter Ecosystem is in the following pages.

The GlobeTrotter Ecosystem

Imagine a world without corruption, abuse of power, poverty, ruling class, NGOs dictating beliefs and actions, government overreach, deficits, tax evasion, and other negative aspects of the current systems. In such a world, everyone's vote counts, and essential items are always readily available.

This is a real plan for a new global economic, monetary system, and everything else system.

NEW ECONOMIC AND MONETARY SYSTEM

Abstract

The current economic system is plagued with problems such as corruption, inequality, poverty, deficits, and abuse of power. To address these issues, a new economic system with universal basic income and jobs (UBIJ) is proposed. The UBIJ system aims to eliminate poverty, reduce inequality, and provide a guaranteed income to every person above the age of 5 in the world, independent of any government or person.

The solution

The proposed system involves the creation of a new global currency, controlled not by any individual or institution, but by everyone. The currency would run on a hybrid blockchain assisted by artificial intelligence, ensuring security and speed without the need for excessive power consumption. The UBIJ system would allow the entire world to receive a basic income without any government falling short of resources or going into debt.

What is UBIJ?

UBIJ is a guaranteed income for every person above the age of 5 in the world, along with job creation for adults and young adults who want to work. It is designed to address the challenges arising from automation and artificial intelligence, which are expected to eliminate many jobs. UBIJ is not limited to any particular country, ensuring that everyone receives it regardless of location.

Benefits of UBIJ

By providing a guaranteed income, UBIJ aims to eliminate poverty and reduce inequality. Additionally, it ensures that people can survive in a world where automation and artificial intelligence are rapidly changing the job market. The UBIJ system also levels the playing field for everyone, taking away the power of the elites and putting them on the same level as everyone else.

Implementation

Once a person reaches the age of 5, they will automatically start receiving UBIJ. The system would not be controlled by any government or individual, ensuring that everyone receives it equally, regardless of location. The UBIJ system would also encourage governments to prioritize the happiness of their residents, as they would have to ensure that their residents are satisfied to retain their wealth in their country.

How is UBIJ possible

With the current political and financial system, it is impossible. The only logical and intelligent way to do it is through a secure blockchain with a set of specific cryptocurrencies. Not just any blockchain or cryptocurrencies; the GlobeTrotter hybrid blockchain assisted by artificial intelligence, that can oversee the volume of transactions and security necessary to handle the whole World at the same time with a group of cryptocurrencies that include a stable coin and specialty tokens.

The new system would create and finance more local jobs like farmers, bakers, plumbers, mom & pop shops, etc. We would get back to basics where everybody can feel more fulfilled and useful again. Being a volunteer worker will be simpler now, helping people that need it thanks to **UBIJ**.

Which currency would be used and what is it backed by?

The main currency would be the GlobeTrotter Globie **GTC** coin (Ǥ) cryptocurrency along with a few other GlobeTrotter specialty tokens (details further down). The Globie could be backed by all the land in the world if it is decided that it needs to be backed by something.

What are the benefits of a Basic Income?

- **Eliminates the "unemployment trap".** Under current systems, when someone gets a job they lose most of their welfare payments. This means they can go from not working at all to working a full week without significantly increasing their income. This is a disincentive to work. Under basic income, when people get a job, they would retain the same basic income payment, with their salary added to it, so the disincentive no longer exists.

- **Reduces government bureaucracy.** A lot of government workers are required to ensure that welfare recipients are not claiming their benefits fraudulently, and to administer the complicated system of welfare payments and tax credits. The increased need for personal tax advisers also sucks skilled workers out of the productive sector. A basic income would hugely simplify the welfare system by replacing most of these bureaucracies, which would reduce its administrative costs significantly.

- **Ends personal taxes.** Taxes are too complicated and costly. Everything we can do to eliminate them would be, all things equal, a net gain in the value of human society. Predicting what tax bracket, you'll be in will no longer be necessary since personal income taxes will no longer exist for most people. Only the very rich will be paying personal taxes (a hoarding tax on their savings).

- **Drop sales tax.** There would only be sales tax on luxury items. There would not be any sales tax on any products or services that are included in basic needs for everyone. If people want and can afford luxury items, then they can afford the taxes.

- **Exemplifies and emphasizes single-class policymaking.** It is not structurally optimal to produce policies that explicitly divide people up into classes and then apply different laws to each class, as the bracketed tax code does (and as the welfare structure does). It is better to form a single law that applies to every individual on the planet: "Everyone gets $x in basic income, funded by a y% flat tax on companies". When we are all in the same 'group', class divisions become less divisive, and we reinforce the principles of liberty and equality.

- **Greatly reduces fraud/waste/abuse**. When welfare subsidies are contingent on conditions like employment, income level, number of hours worked, family status, etc., there are opportunities to game the system, either by illegally lying (fraud) or by simply obeying the economic incentives put in front of you (waste/abuse). These cause losses of real economic value, which are paid for by every taxpayer. Removing this incentive structure allows confidence in the welfare system's ability to reach people exactly as intended.

- **Guarantees a minimum living standard.** Though it's subjective/politicized, people may be entitled to a certain basic standard of living, regardless of whether they are momentarily able to participate in the labor market. Universal Declaration of Human Rights, Article 25, states, "Everyone has the right to a standard of living adequate for the health and well-being of himself and of his family, including food, clothing, housing and medical care and necessary social services, and the right to security in the event of unemployment, sickness, disability, widowhood, old age or other lack of livelihood in circumstances beyond his control." (United Nations, (UN)).

- **Increases bargaining power for workers.** Workers will be able to afford to refuse a job if the employer abuses its "cartel-like mindset" or the workspace has poor conditions, so firms will be forced to improve the employment conditions and wages for their workers. This will happen as a natural result of negotiation between firms and workers and will not require government intervention or unionization.

- **Lowers need for government regulations on the labor market.** Policies such as the minimum wage will become less necessary with the basic income, as people will already get enough money to live on from the basic income. And negotiating power for workers will increase. This will allow the government to remove some of the regulations on the labor market, creating a freer market and providing benefits for both employers and employees.

- **Deters undocumented immigration.** With the minimum wage obsolete, manual labor can be priced at its fair-market value, meaning undocumented immigrants will have to accept even lower wages to compensate for their legal risks, potentially putting the standard of life lower than if they stayed where they were.

- **Reduces the gender "pay gap".** Women, on average, make less money than men, and debaters of this issue fall into two camps: (1) those who want to reduce that gap to help women achieve financial freedom, and (2) those who want to prevent the harmful effects of government pay-mandates and micromanagement. Basic Income is capable of satisfying both camps by giving all citizens a base income, making women (and people in general) less dependent on their work-income. And it does so without removing any of the beneficial capitalistic incentives to work and provide value. Furthermore, the gender pay gap is reduced for precisely those women who most need it: low-income women. It makes them less dependent on a potentially abusive spouse and less sensitive to pregnancy-based work issues, without unjustly interfering with the market's ability to set salaries for upper and middle-class workers.

- **Improves mental health and security.** Mental health is one of the largest public health problems in most developed countries. The knowledge that the basic income will ensure a basic standard of living in any circumstances will provide a sense of mental security, especially when the economy is performing poorly. The removal of various dehumanising tests and stigmatisation of anyone who receives welfare payments will also serve to improve mental health. There is also evidence that poverty itself reduces cognitive capacity, comparable to a loss of 13 IQ points, or chronic alcoholism as compared to sobriety. A basic income would remove this cognitive impairment.

- **Increases physical health.** The rising cost of health care is a cause of great long-term concern, and basic income could lower this cost. In the Dauphin, Manitoba pilot experiment in Canada, an 8.5% reduction in hospitalization was found to be a direct result of the minimum income. This was attributed to the reduction in workplace injuries and family violence resulting from the rise in incomes.

- **Stabilizes costs over time.** Current welfare schemes have costs that fluctuate significantly with the performance of the economy and are increasing as the populations ages and more people leave the workforce. The costs of basic income schemes would not see this fluctuation, as the basic income is paid to all people* regardless of whether they are in the labor force or not.

- **Deals better with widespread unemployment.** Some people may argue that, with the development of new automation technology and the increase in the labour force due to globalisation, rates of unemployment in developed countries are likely to stay high and increase in coming years. This would impose a significant increased cost on current schemes, but as spending from the basic income would not increase, this system would be more able to cope with the change. Also, the long stressful wait to receive your first unemployment check would be eliminated.

- **Redistributes money from capital to labor.** Even if technology doesn't lead to high unemployment, it may well lead to lower wages and greater inequality. Capital, equipment and machinery that helps to produce things, is now creating a greater share of output compared to labour; human workers. This allows business owners, who own the capital, to pay workers the same or less while more is produced, so they make more profit for themselves. We are already seeing that output per worker is increasing, while workers' wages are not. In the long term, this will mean that business owners make more and more money, while those who don't own capital will make less and less. Basic income alleviates this by taxing the companies and the rich (who will probably own capital) and giving money to the poor (who probably won't), even if they can't find a job.

- **Increases number of small businesses.** Many people may currently be discouraged from leaving their job to start their own business, as if the venture fails, they will have no source of income. The basic income would provide income to these people, so more people would feel able to start businesses which could only increase innovation and competition in the economy. Evidence of this effect can be found in the Namibia basic income experiment, where those receiving it showed an increase in entrepreneurship with a 29% increase in average earned income, excluding the basic income. At the beginning of **UBIJ**, every adult will receive a big amount of "money" to help start a business if they wish. Every other person will also receive this, one-time, big amount once they reach adulthood.

- **Increases charitable work and academic research.** Much work in the charitable sector and other vocations (e.g., open-source programming, academia, or the arts) is socially beneficial but not profitable, so people have to do it in their spare time, along with a traditional job. A basic income would allow these people to spend more time on work that is socially beneficial but normally unprofitable for the individual.

- **Increases number of people in jobs they enjoy.** As people will not be forced to take on a job, they will be more able to find a job that they enjoy (or that pays well enough to offset their lack of enjoyment). Having people in jobs that suit them better will help improve mental health, as well as leading to an improved quality of goods and services.

- **Gives financial independence to all adults.** Every adult will be entitled to the basic income independently of any other people. This means they cannot be controlled or manipulated by someone through control of their finances, allowing people in abusive relationships to escape them more easily.

- **Helps families be happier and more independent.** The first two children of each family will also receive UBIJ to help pay for their needs without weighing on the family unit. Half of the UBIJ will be available for the parents to use for their children and the other half will be frozen until the children are 16 and old enough to manage their own finances.

- **Prevents generational theft.** Most western countries already provide basic income to people of retired age. But, if a nation or its socialized retirement program goes bankrupt or the socialized retirement program otherwise becomes unaffordable (most likely within 10 years due to fiscal mismanagement or simple birth rate demographics), then it is to the great advantage of current benefit recipients and at the total cost to those who pay into the benefits today with the false promise of receiving them in the future. If entitlements are unaffordable/unsustainable, then the only fair solution is to provide the funds equally today.

- **Leverages the multiplier effect.** "The mechanism that can give rise to a multiplier effect is that an initial incremental amount of spending can lead to increased consumption spending, increasing income further and hence further increasing consumption, etc., resulting in an overall increase in national income greater than the initial incremental amount of spending." It is this same effect that is seen in the differences to the economy the effects of $1 being spent by high income earners versus low-income earners have. As published in a recent report, "All those dollars low-wage workers spend create an economic ripple effect. Every extra dollar going into the pockets of low-wage workers, standard economic multiplier models tell us, adds about $1.21 to the national economy. Every extra dollar going into the pockets of a high-income American, by contrast, only adds about 39 cents to the GDP." This means a basic income could show this same multiplier effect on the entire economy by redistributing money from high earners to low and middle earners where the effects of spending are amplified.

Programs that could be cut with UBIJ

Some programs could be cut because of **UBIJ** but the moneys saved will be able to be put to better use. Governments will be getting the necessary amounts every month to supply all the benefits they need to offer their citizens, so these services are no longer needed:

- Welfare/workfare
- Business tax deductions/credits/subsidies
- Unemployment insurance

- Government pensions
- National minimum wage laws

HOW THIS WILL WORK

Who will receive UBIJ?

We will be giving every adult in the World ₲10,000 Globies in the beginning (or on their 18th birthday), then ₲1500 per month. There will be ₲300 per month to every young person between the ages of 5 and 17.

How this will be funded

- By charging a 30% tax to EVERY business in the World (25% going for **UBIJ** and 5% going to the local governments). Thus, eliminating any tax havens and companies moving out of a country because they can pay less elsewhere.
- By charging a 15% tax on luxury items going right to the local governments.
- By having a 10% hoarding tax on savings thus charging 10% on any savings (for individuals & companies) over a certain amount (like ₲1,000,000?) (Going to **UBIJ**).
- By having a 25% tax on any currency coming into a wallet (over a certain amount and a limited number of deposits that isn't from a regular income like from **UBIJ** or a regular salary under a certain amount) like big gifts, inheritances, winnings, etc. (20% for **UBIJ** and 5% for governments).
- By renting out all land worldwide and putting all the money back into the **UBIJ** system.

What security measures would be taken to make it tamper proof?

- The whole system will be automated on a hybrid blockchain, uncontrollable and unstoppable by any government or person.

- Everybody on the planet will be issued a unique ID kept private on the hybrid blockchain using a multimodal biometric identification.
- The system will run itself and not be influenced by anybody or any government without a proper vote.
- There will be a Justice Force that will take care of anybody abusing the system or stealing from others. Again, everything will be by vote on the blockchain. It will be instant justice, no more courts to slow the process down or let the rich & powerful get away with things they shouldn't. Nobody will be immune to the Justice Force.

What will happen with the banks?

- Every central, public and private bank on the planet can and will be shut down and used for something else.
- Every person's bank account will have the amount recorded just before the official announcement of **UBIJ** and people will receive the equal amount to what they were holding in the bank. There will be safeguards in place so that they cannot claim more coins than they should.

What about inflation?

Since every business will be accepting Globies, they will need to have a wallet and an API for their systems. Every API will have a serial number and will be controlled by the blockchain which in turn is controlled by the general population through voting. If companies abuse the system or exaggerate, people can vote and have that company's ability to accept tokens suspended, taxed or even shut down if it happens often enough. This system will give back the power to the people where it belongs. Since there will be less people working, more machines, and other factors, inflation will be not non-existent. Machines do not require more money and people should be paid the same amount for doing the same job. Any increase in salary should come from profit sharing or a new higher position.

Inflation is a by-product of greed and wanting more for doing the same job and governments printing money like there is no tomorrow.

The consequences of having the Globie as the global currency

If everyone and every government on the planet agreed to use the Globie for trade, it would have significant implications for the global economy and financial systems. Here are some potential consequences:

1. **Universal acceptance:** With global agreement, the Globie would become a universally accepted medium of exchange. This could simplify international trade, reducing the need for currency conversions and associated fees.

2. **No transaction costs:** Cryptocurrencies generally offer lower transaction fees compared to traditional payment systems and the Globie would have no fees. Universal adoption would lead to significant cost savings for businesses and consumers for transactions including in cross-border transactions.

3. **Increased financial inclusion:** The Globie can provide access to financial services for people who are unbanked or underbanked, particularly in developing countries. A universally accepted cryptocurrency like the Globie would further promote financial inclusion.

4. **Enhanced security and privacy:** The Globie which is based on blockchain technology, offers increased security and privacy compared to traditional financial systems. Universal adoption could lead to more secure transactions and financial privacy for users.

5. **Greater transparency:** The Globie offers a high level of transparency since transactions are recorded on a public ledger. This could reduce corruption and improve trust in the global financial system.

6. **Monetary policy implications:** If the Globie were to replace all national currencies, governments would lose control over monetary policy. This could have positive implications. On one hand, it could eliminate the risk of currency manipulation and inflation caused by government policies. Plus, it would limit governments' ability to overspend.

7. **Economic power shifts:** The widespread adoption of the Globie could shift economic power away from countries that currently have dominant currencies (such as the United States and the European Union). This could have geopolitical implications and affect international relations in a positive way.

8. **Decentralization:** By removing control from central banks and governments, the Globie would lead to a more decentralized financial system, making it more resistant to manipulation and corruption.

9. **No more inflation:** The Globie with a predetermined and transparent monetary policy would help eliminate the risk of inflation, as the money supply would be more predictable and not subject to government intervention.

10. **Empowerment of individuals:** A decentralized financial system could empower individuals by giving them more control over their finances and the ability to vote on important matters through blockchain technology.

11. **Efficient markets:** We could eliminate bailouts. Without government bailouts, failing businesses would not be artificially propped up, potentially leading to more efficient markets where resources are allocated based on merit and performance.

12. **Eliminate tax evasion:** A transparent and traceable Globie would make it impossible for individuals and businesses to evade taxes, resulting in increased government revenue.

13. **Universal Basic Income (UBI):** The Globie system would incorporate a mechanism for providing UBI, ensuring a basic level of financial security for all individuals worldwide.

14. **Better allocation of government resources:** With increased revenue from reduced tax evasion, governments might have more funds available to allocate towards social programs, infrastructure, and other public goods.

15. **Financial inclusion:** The Globie with UBI could further promote financial inclusion by providing access to basic financial resources for people in developing countries or those who were unbanked.

16. **Reduced income inequality:** The implementation of UBI and more equitable access to financial resources could help reduce income inequality and promote economic mobility.

17. **Stimulating economic growth:** By providing a stable, secure, and transparent financial system, the Globie would encourage investment and trade, fostering global economic growth.

18. **Enhanced government transparency:** A global cryptocurrency could improve transparency in government spending, making it easier for citizens to hold their governments accountable for the allocation of public funds.

19. **Environmental benefits:** If the hybrid blockchain technology used for the Globie addresses energy consumption concerns, the system could potentially have a lower environmental impact compared to traditional financial systems and some existing cryptocurrencies.

THE GLOBETROTTER BENEFITS

Wallet

Each individual wallet will be held on a mobile phone or tablet. Most people will have their wallet on their mobile phone and most companies will probably have their wallet on a tablet or computer. The balance is always in the wallet so no matter what, you always have all your money with you. The phone will update the blockchain every time it connects to the internet. The phone and the blockchain will do their checks and balances to make sure everything balances. The business wallets will be able to have multiple users, each using their own ID to make transactions for the company. This way, everybody knows what everybody else is doing in the company. The private transactions will not be available for companies.

A lost phone does not mean a lost wallet. If lost, getting a new phone, and setting it up with your biometrics means your wallet is automatically updated on your new phone with the same quantity of tokens you had in the old phone but all new tokens and coins whereas the old ones are burned on the blockchain. If just changing phones, you will be able to transfer all the tokens from the old phone to the new one.

Eliminating personal income tax

This system will allow the governments to receive more than enough coins from the taxes collected from the businesses and luxury taxes to cover all expenses thus eliminating personal income taxes for all. Plus, governments are able to keep their different programs running. The people are the ones that will be voting on how and where that tax money is spent.

The 5% taxes collected from the businesses and individuals getting big amounts (that are not **UBIJ** or salaries) and the 15% luxury tax, will go to the government where the people are registered as residing. This should eliminate illegal immigrants since everybody is getting money and it is in the country's best interest to let as many people register in their country as possible. Governments will be making their countries more attractive to foreigners and doing everything they can to keep the residents they have, happy.

Past Debt

Debt is not real since the banks created "money" out of thin air so every debt to any financial institution in the World will be erased. People will no longer owe money to banks or credit card companies for anything they own. Future debt will only be allowed up to a certain percentage of income. Every business in the World will be able to accept Lay-a-way plans. People need to live within their means which will only make people healthier and happier not having the weight of debt always on their minds.

GlobeTrotter Credit Cards

GlobeTrotter will give out credit cards to people 16 years old and older. They will come with a low maximum credit amount and will be able to go higher if the system deems the holder capable and responsible enough. The payments will be taken automatically every month by smart contract directly from their **UBIJ**. GlobeTrotter will teach everybody responsible spending and saving. There will be no interest charges on the credit nor any charges to the merchants accepting the Credit Cards.

Energy Companies

To promote a more equitable energy system, it is proposed that every energy company, including those that provide gas, oil, electric power, and other forms of energy, should become publicly owned and operated. This would ensure that prices are fair, while still allowing the company to make a reasonable profit that can be put back into the UBIJ system.

This proposal seeks to address the issue of companies that took advantage of people before, as they will no longer exist under this system. These companies will not be compensated for their businesses since they have already exploited the planet's resources and profited from something that did not belong to them in the first place. This approach aims to promote a more ethical and sustainable energy system that benefits everyone, rather than a select few.

Loans

Private loans between individuals will be possible with a maximum of 5% yearly interest.

If the loan was for building a business and the owner defaults on the loan, the business would belong to the lender, but the lender would have to pay a certain amount of what he received back to the borrower. The two parties will be able to negotiate a new contract if they wish to continue the arrangement.

If the loan is for a service business, artist or invention, the borrower will need to put up collateral for the loan or workout a deal of a % of every sale through a smart contract. If the borrower defaults, the lender would become half owner of whatever was being made.

Unique ID system

GlobeTrotter will give a smartphone to everyone that needs one. We will offer everybody on the planet a chance to get their own official ID, free of charge, to be able to receive their **UBIJ** payments and participate in any government programs available to them using their phone. The system will use a combination of face, retina, and fingerprint recognition and be updated every 5 years on their birthday.

Each person will need 1 person to vouch for them and be responsible for them. People cannot vouch for each other. One person cannot vouch for more than 20 people.

There will be information needed to make sure that everybody is known. There will be no secret identities and anybody wanting to collect **UBIJ**, or even use the GlobeTrotter system, will need to prove their identity.

At birth, the two parents (or the doctor and one parent) will create a new wallet for the child and at one year old, the child, with the help of his parent(s) will be required to input the necessary biometrics into his/her wallet.

Death and leaving your estate to others

When a person is living, they will be asked to choose a person as their executor. That executor will receive a special Executor token. When a person dies, a coroner will send a special token to the wallet of the dead person indicating that the owner is dead. The wallet will then reach out to the executor and ask for the Executor token. Now, the executor will have access to the deceased person's wallet.

Voting System (accountability)

The voting system will be available to everyone. It will be for voting on:

- Abusers*
- Companies that are charging too much or acting poorly
- Improvements on the system
- How and where taxes are spent by the governments
- People that aren't bringing anything positive to the community/World
- And many other things

*The people will also decide on the punishment through voting.

Voters will get paid for voting.

The benefits of this system

- Limiting the number of homes, a person or company can own.
- Being able to regulate big tech companies like Facebook, Twitter, Google, and others.
- Eliminating lobbying.
- Being able to fine, limit or close a company that abuses or endangers people or the environment.
- **Give a phone to everyone that needs one and expand wireless internet service Worldwide and having every blockchain transaction be free of charge (no internet fee).**
- Strengthen antitrust standards for companies.

- Limit markup prices.
- Eliminating discrimination and racism through education.
- No more need for passports.
- No more subsidies, government contracts, sub-contracting for governments (No more: private jails/prisons, schools for profit, private healthcare, etc.).
- Governments will run the businesses that supply essential services (Health care, schooling, cable tv, phone service, food markets, clothing manufacturers, etc.).
- No more supreme court as we know it.
- No more stock markets as we know them. They will be replaced with something else, but all the shares will be non-voting and the share holders have NO influence over the company. Companies cannot buy back their shares and the number of shares (of a certain company) per wallet will be limited.
- The percentage of extra taxes a company pays will be in ratio with the difference between the CEO/owner's pay and the typical worker's pay.
- The investment portfolios will be taxed every year on the value of it at that time.
- Regulate ALL markets; like no more than 10% profits for anything health related or anything essential.

Problems that would be solved

- No more cryptocurrency volatility.
- No more credit card frauds.
- No more ESG nonsense.
- No more climate change scare tactics.
- No more corrupt government officials.
- No more malfeasance, bribery, kickbacks influence-peddling.
- No more governments telling people what to do.
- No more problems for whistle blowers.

- No more election fraud.
- No more foreign governments causing problems in other countries.
- No more need for tariffs.
- No more corrupt justice officials.
- No more organized crime syndicates.
- No more terrorist groups like Antifa or BLM.
- No more tax evasion possible for companies.
- No more ruining the environment.
- No more raping the natural resources.
- No need for central banks or any banks for that matter.
- No more money laundering.
- No more terrorist financing.
- No more Jails.
- No more tax breaks for the rich and the big corporations.
- No more subsidies for companies/industries that don't really need them. If they can't compete within a free market, too bad.
- No more bank frauds.
- No more interest rate manipulations.
- No more mortgages and large debts.
- No more forex frauds or manipulations.
- No more governments spying on their citizens.
- No more sweatshops.
- No more CIA, FBI, NSA and all other "security" organizations and worldwide equivalents.
- **No more WARS**.
- No more spending on the military.
- No more armies.
- Free commuting on buses and trains
- Free schooling for life and all schools are non-profit
- Free childcare
- Free healthcare

- All salaries, incomes and expenditures will be public on the blockchain. This should cut down on inequality
- And the list goes on…

Open markets

There can be a return of real open markets. People will have the possibility of voting for what they want available or banned in their city, state, country, World. People caught selling or bringing in unwanted products/services in a protected area will be penalized. There will be designated areas for drugs, prostitution, and gambling. People will be allowed to go there BUT every expenditure made there will be visible on the blockchain.

Innovation

Innovation will be encouraged by granting free international patents to everyone that has an idea/invention that qualifies. 20% of their royalties will be going back into the **UBIJ**. Every patent will be on a smart contract and people will be automatically paid for the use of their ideas.

Abusers

Abusers will be voted against by their peers. The punishments can be anywhere from a fine to being banned from a country, or worse if they are proven to not bring anything positive to the society. It will start with the person paying back double what they took, back to the people involved. Then, after another abuse, maybe shipped to a country/island with other abusers (to be determined and voted on).

Governments abusing in any way will be voted on and can be removed from power. If individuals in government are voted guilty, they will be treated like any other abuser. There will be no one above the rules or the punishments.

Future Jobs

We don't know what the future holds but one thing is for sure, there will be less jobs because of AI and automation. There will always be a need for people in certain jobs and because of **UBIJ**, the job perks will need to be good and the bosses as well since the people will have the luxury of being able to refuse a job.

The initial payment from **UBIJ** should be enough to help start many small local businesses and create jobs.

Relief Funds

Relief funds will be always available to help areas that have been hit by natural disasters or because of human destruction. These funds will be voted on by everyone.

Land

THE PLANET BELONGS TO EVERYBODY. No person or government really owns any land. This way, there will be no more land ownership for anybody. Anybody living on a piece of land will pay rent to the rest of the World for that piece of land for his or her dwelling/business/usage of it. People lease the land from the planet (**UBIJ**) and can only sell what they have built or improved on the land. All leases would be put up for vote through a smart contract and if people do not respect their smart contract, they lose the use of the land and their deposit. Existing ownership will be recognized as a 100-year lease. The piece of land can never be sold, only the property that is built on it.

Land rental price will depend on what it will be used for, size and natural resources. People that used to work in certain positions in the government but are no longer needed because of **UBIJ**, will be able to continue working and evaluating land for the rental price.

Housing

Homes will be built for everyone by the **UBIJ** system, thus creating jobs, and these homes will be on a rent-to-own basis and the rental income will be used for building new homes. There will be a maximum number of homes a person or company can own thus ending any control issues.

Rental prices for other buildings not owned by the **UBIJ** system will be governed and regulated as to control landlords that typically abuse their power. Any landlord caught neglecting and/or abusing will face consequences.

Natural resources

Land will be leased to excavation companies through voting. Anybody excavating land for the natural resources needs to respect the environment otherwise they lose the right to excavate and the right to rent any other piece of land. The piece of land that is being used needs to be better than when the excavating company first got there.

Governments

All governments will go back to the way they were meant; to serve the public and take care of things that we do not want to do or have time to do.

Since everything will be simplified, governments can be downsized and become more efficient.

The differences between today's blockchain systems and the GlobeTrotter system

Cryptocurrencies and blockchains are the future and are greatly needed and have many upsides to them but they have their down sides too. Here, we will address how GlobeTrotter Cryptocurrency will resolve these problems.

Adoption by the masses

Right now, people are mostly using cryptocurrencies for speculation and investment purposes. Cryptocurrencies are too volatile for merchants to accept and possibly too profitable as an investment for consumers to use.

The solution is a stable cryptocurrency, and the GlobeTrotter Globie coin is the only truly stable coin. It will be attractive to both merchants and consumers because of it always having the exact same value. This is the key to a cryptocurrency being adopted and used by the masses.

Difficult to understand

There is a big learning curve to understanding and using cryptocurrency. Things need to be more user friendly and intuitive.

GlobeTrotter will have a simple to use interface that will feel familiar to people. Straightforward, simple, and logical.

The loss of wallets

People losing their wallets (for reasons like hacks, computer crash, losing their computer or phone, etc.) are a reality and a big downside right now.

GlobeTrotter will have a backup system in place to recover lost wallets and private keys. This is something that is easily implemented and greatly needed in the cryptocurrency world.

The loss of funds

People and businesses being hacked happens. Right now, anybody that loses their coins from being hacked doesn't have the chance of getting them back. Once they are gone, they are gone for good.

GlobeTrotter will have a system that will let them block the stolen coins from being used and replace them back to the original owners. Through our PIN system, the stolen coins are rendered useless without the PIN number and it also gives us time to blacklist the stolen coins in case they can crack the PIN number.

Government/Police Seizure Protection

Illegal government and police seizures are a very real possibility. Many countries like the USA have "legalized" illegal seizures of property. With the new laws saying that you have to declare carrying over $10,000 worth of cryptocurrency when entering the country, they can seize it if you don't declare it and even if you declare it. Technically, nobody can carry cryptocurrency, it's on the blockchain, but that won't stop them.

Our wallets will have a pin number that is required to open it. They will also have an emergency pin number that, if entered, will show your balance as whatever you want it to.

Purchase protection

When purchasing something online with cryptocurrency, you need to completely trust the merchant because once you send him your coins, they are his and if he doesn't send you the product, you lose.

GlobeTrotter has developed their "Smarter Contract System" that will let consumers easily create a contract that if not respected by the merchant, they are refunded. This new system eliminates possibilities of fraud.

Scalability

Most blockchains have scaling issues which result in slower confirmation times as it gets busier. The more people on a blockchain, the slower it gets and the more expensive it gets.

GlobeTrotter's hybrid blockchain (T-Chain) will be the opposite. The more people use it, the faster and more secure it gets. Through our combination of different technologies, we plan to solve every problem present blockchains are having. This "T-Chain" is the ultimate decentralized solution.

No real advantages in purchasing with cryptocurrencies today

Right now, there aren't really any advantages to purchasing anything with cryptocurrency. It won't cost you anything less and most merchants that do accept cryptos go through a third party like Coinbase to transfer the purchase to FIAT currency and pay fees.

GlobeTrotter will not charge any fees when paying with or transferring Globies.

Developers and miners

Every cryptocurrency and blockchain is dependent on the developers and miners and when those two disagree, there is a fork. That affects the value of the coins/tokens and we can only sit back and watch.

The GlobeTrotter Ecosystem will be the way it should have been from the start. There will be no possibility of a fork. Anything added to the system will be voted on by all token holders and anything that is put up for vote can only have upsides. It is especially important to GlobeTrotter that everybody always comes out ahead.

Debit cards

Right now, there are dozens of cryptocurrency debit cards but they aren't really solving any problems. They actually cost the consumer more than using a bank debit card and the merchants still have to pay the same fees. One important reason for cryptocurrency's reason for being is to cut out the middleman. These debit cards are just middlemen on a blockchain. Plus, who really wants to spend a coin that is going up in value? Almost nobody.

GlobeTrotter eliminates the need for debit cards. Everything will be on your phone.

Privacy

Most blockchains show every transaction on them and even though it is wallet number to wallet number and there are no names attached to any of them, most remain traceable by people who know what they are doing. Not everybody wants that info out there so GlobeTrotter has added a privacy option on every transaction through its "Smarter Contract System." It lets only the two people involved in the transaction to be able to view it on the T-Chain. There will be a limit on how many private transactions you can have. Only a member of the Justice Force will have access to the private transaction but only with serious doubts of elicit behaviour.

Big ICO's slowing down the blockchains and making coins even more volatile

The problem with big ICO's is that they slow down the blockchains of the participating cryptocurrencies. Also, when all those buyers are acquiring coins to buy into the ICO's, the price goes up and when comes time for those ICO's to cash out, they make the market drop again creating a very volatile scenario.

With the Globie coin, ICO's will be able to collect funds that will always have the same value. No worries of it dropping in value overnight. If the ICO's use Globie coins instead of BTC, ETH or any other, they won't be overloading those blockchains and it will also help in stabilizing those coins plus, there are no fees.

Smart Contracts

Smart contracts are fantastic, and their usefulness is endless but to make smart contracts right now, you need to be a programmer in that language. To use smart contracts, you need to write one or refer to an existing one on the blockchain. There are millions of possibilities to have in smart contracts so keeping track of all of them is nearly impossible.

GlobeTrotters' solution is simpler. Every token has a smart contract embedded into it. Using the GlobeTrotter Wallet with the "Smarter Contract System" built into it, you can create a smart contract as easily as checking off whichever conditions you want on the list, adding dates and times and more. This lets you include any condition you want for the transaction to be complete. The receiver will see a copy of the contract and have the choice to accept it, refuse it or suggest changes.

THE TECHNOLOGY

The blockchain

The blockchain will be a hybrid blockchain by using the best of a decentralized and private blockchain technology to create a super secure and super fast 100% decentralized blockchain. This blockchain cannot be manipulated by outside forces other than everything being voted on by the citizens of the World. There will be fail-safes in place as to not be able to vote for a higher UBI wage for everyone UNLESS the system can afford it over time, and other contingencies. The blockchain will be assisted by artificial intelligence. The blockchain will be free to use, meaning no cost to make any transactions or transfers.

The crypto tokens and coins

- **GTC coin:** This coin (Globie) will be the currency used for all purchases. It will have a constant value because there will no longer be any inflation. There will be a limited amount of GTC coins in the system albeit a huge number of them.

- **GTP token:** This NFT token will be used for property ownership and transfers. Anybody will be able to mint a GTP with their property token and transfer their property to the blockchain if wanted where it can be kept, sold, or traded.

- **GTV token:** This NFT token will be used for voting. Everybody will receive a bunch of tokens for voting. These tokens will represent each individual. This way, the blockchain knows who owns the token and each person can only vote once per vote. This token is not transferable to others. Once a voting token is used, it is burned.

- **GTA token:** This NFT token will be used for admissions to replace tickets. Venues with shows or admittance requirements will mint GTA tokens to sell them or give them away.

- **GGT token:** This NFT token will be used as a gift token or a coupon token. Its purpose will be for promotional use for gifts, rewards, bonuses, etc. Each business will be able to mint them for their own business and send them out to whoever or give them out on their website.

- **GTE token:** This NFT token will be used to choose an executor. This token can only be sent back to the original owner. If the holder dies, the GTE token will be automatically sent back to the original owner.

- **GTI token:** This NFT token will be used as an ID token whenever you need to send someone your details or prove who you are. This token would be used when creating a new wallet for a newborn among other things, open an account, or retrieve an account.

The Smarter Contract System

Every coin/token will have a "Smarter Contract" imbedded into it to let the users define the conditions when sending and/or receiving them. The "Smarter Contracts" are part of the coin and not a separate entity on the blockchain like most other smart contracts. Why "Smarter Contract"? Because it is extremely simple to use and a smarter way to use smart contracts. To define what the conditions that need to be fulfilled are for the coins, the user will just need to check off the desired choices from a list. It will be an extremely user-friendly system.

<u>**Security**</u>

Unlike all cryptocurrencies today, if the wallet or private keys are lost, they will be recoverable. If the wallet is hacked and coins/tokens are stolen without the smarter contract being filled out (which only the owner can do), they will be recovered and placed back into your wallet.

There will be many safeguards in the system making it impossible to steal coins. Also, the smarter contracts will eliminate chargebacks protecting the merchants from fraud.

THE REFORM OF MOST INDUSTRIES

<u>STOCK MARKETS</u>

Stock markets will be eliminated all together and replaced with a more equitable system that cannot be manipulated. The stock markets were created by the rich **FOR** the rich just to further their wealth by cheating the system. The stock markets no longer have anything to do with reality. The stock markets will be replaced by a new system that will use strict rules that everyone will have to follow being that it will run on the blockchain and there will be no way to cheat or fix the system.

- **Immutable and Transparent Transactions:**

The new stock market systems will leverage the power of blockchain technology to ensure all transactions are recorded in an immutable and transparent manner. Every trade will be permanently stored on the blockchain, providing a comprehensive and auditable transaction history.

- **Smart Contracts for Compliance:**

Compliance with regulatory requirements will be enforced through smart contracts deployed on the blockchain. These self-executing contracts will automatically validate and enforce compliance rules, ensuring fair and consistent treatment of market participants.

- **Decentralized Governance and Voting:**

A decentralized governance model will be implemented, allowing market participants to actively participate in decision-making processes. Through secure voting mechanisms on the blockchain, stakeholders will collectively determine rules, punishments, and regulatory changes.

- **Whistleblower Protection:**

The new system will prioritize the protection of whistleblowers by employing advanced cryptographic techniques and pseudonymity. Whistleblowers will be able to report misconduct anonymously, ensuring their safety while providing critical information for investigations.

- **Immutable Complaint System:**

A transparent and immutable complaint system will be integrated into the blockchain platform. This system will securely record and track complaints, ensuring transparency, accountability, and fairness in addressing grievances and disputes.

- **Global Economic System:**

A unified global economic system will be established on the blockchain, featuring a single currency for seamless cross-border transactions. This system will foster economic integration and stability, eliminating complexities associated with multiple currencies.

- **Efficient Dispute Resolution:**

Dispute resolution processes will be streamlined through the use of smart contracts and decentralized arbitration mechanisms. The blockchain's immutable records and tamper-resistant nature will ensure fair and efficient resolution of conflicts.

- **AI-Powered Market Surveillance:**

Advanced AI algorithms will be employed for real-time market surveillance, detecting patterns of market manipulation, insider trading, and fraudulent activities. AI will act as a vigilant overseer, ensuring market integrity and investor protection.

- **AI-Driven Risk Assessment:**

AI models will assess and quantify risks associated with different investments, portfolios, and market conditions. Investors will benefit from personalized risk analysis, empowering them to make well-informed investment decisions.

- **AI-Enabled Investor Education:**

AI-powered educational tools and platforms will provide personalized investment guidance, empowering investors with knowledge and insights tailored to their individual profiles. This AI-driven education will foster financial literacy and responsible investment practices.

- **AI-Enhanced Market Efficiency:**

AI algorithms will optimize trade execution, improving liquidity and reducing transaction costs. By analyzing market data and participant behavior, AI will enhance market efficiency and promote fair and timely trade execution.

- **AI-Powered Investor Protection:**

AI models will proactively identify and flag potential investor vulnerabilities, providing early warning systems for scams or fraudulent schemes. This AI-powered investor protection will safeguard individuals from financial exploitation.

EDUCATIONAL SYSTEM

- **An Emphasis on Factual Learning & Intellectual Freedom:**

Discarding divisive and counterproductive ideologies such as DEI programs, loyalty tests, and Critical Race Theory, the revised educational framework will instead promote intellectual freedom and factual learning.

Education should not be about indoctrinating students with a certain worldview, but about expanding their minds and encouraging independent thinking. It is through this emphasis on critical thinking, not what to think, but how to think, that we can mold our future generations into discerning, compassionate, and engaged citizens.

- **Critical Thinking & Logical Reasoning:**

Right from their formative years, students will be immersed in an educational environment that prioritizes the development of critical thinking skills and logical reasoning. Instruction in the principles of logic, the art of reasoning, and the rigours of the scientific method will be integral to their learning journey. They will be equipped to question, to debate, and to evaluate the credibility of sources. This foundational skillset will permeate every subject they tackle, enabling them to critically analyze and scrutinize all information they encounter throughout their lives.

- **Balanced and Inclusive History Curriculum:**

The study of history will take center stage in our proposed curriculum, providing students with a broad understanding of diverse political systems, the intrinsic value of individual freedoms, and the perilous nature of totalitarian regimes. History will not be taught through a narrow, divisive lens, but rather with a focus on shared human experiences and the lessons we can learn from them. The aim is to instil in students an appreciation for democratic, just and fair values and to underscore the pivotal role of vigilant, informed citizenship in safeguarding these liberties.

- **Entrepreneurship & Economic Acumen:**

To cultivate self-reliance and foster a spirit of independence, students will be introduced to the fundamentals of entrepreneurship and economic literacy. They'll gain insights into the intricacies of budgeting, the art of investing, the inescapable reality of taxes, and the foundational elements of initiating and managing a business. These essential, real-world skills will empower them to adeptly steer their financial futures and confidently navigate the economic dimensions of their lives.

- **Practical Self-sufficiency Skills:**

In addition to academic subjects, the curriculum will incorporate practical skills essential for self-sufficiency. This could span from the therapeutic art of gardening, rudimentary home repair techniques, the culinary science of cooking, basic first aid proficiency, to a host of other survival skills. This comprehensive approach aims to equip students with the necessary competencies to be self-sustaining in various facets of life.

- **Promotion of Open Discourse & Debate:**

Classroom environments will be nurtured to foster open discourse and lively debates, providing students with a platform to freely articulate their thoughts and viewpoints. This will cultivate an atmosphere of intellectual curiosity, nudging students to delve into diverse perspectives and formulate their own well-informed opinions.

- **Customized Learning Trajectories:**

Acknowledging the distinctiveness of each student, the educational system will advocate for tailored learning trajectories. This method will enable students to explore their individual interests and talents, thereby kindling a passion for learning and facilitating personal growth.

- **Teacher Training & Support:**

Educators will be provided with comprehensive training to equip them with these novel teaching methodologies and subject matter. They will also receive continuous support and resources to hone their skills and adapt to the evolving educational landscape. However, educators advocating for transgender ideologies and similar narratives will no longer be permitted in the educational system.

- **Whole-Person Development:**

The educational system should cherish and cultivate all facets of a child's development, including their physical health, mental and emotional well-being, social aptitude, artistic creativity, and beyond. This could involve integrating physical education, the arts, mindfulness practices, and more into the day-to-day curriculum.

- **Global Economics & Monetary Acumen:**

In the transformed global economic system with a single currency and no traditional banks, students will be educated on the system's unique dynamics and personal financial management. They'll comprehend how this unified currency impacts worldwide trade, economics, and personal wealth, as well as the influence of economic policies. They'll learn to balance expenses, savings, and investments and understand the significance of secure digital transactions, individual accountability, and transparency in this new system. The goal is to equip them with the skills to make informed decisions that promote their financial stability and positively impact the global community.

FOOD & BEVERAGE INDUSTRY

- **Transparency in Labeling:**

Consumers should know exactly what they're eating. Implement stricter regulations on food and beverage labeling to ensure that all ingredients are listed clearly and accurately. This includes potentially harmful additives, preservatives, and artificial flavors or colors. A traffic light system could be introduced on packaging to indicate the healthiness of the product.

- **Encourage Local and Seasonal Produce:**

Promote the use of local, seasonal produce in food production. This not only reduces the environmental footprint of food transport but also tends to result in fresher and more nutritious products. Government incentives could be provided to businesses that source locally.

- **Eliminate Harmful Substances:**

Phase out the use of harmful substances such as trans fats, high-fructose corn syrup, and certain artificial sweeteners in food and beverage production. Establish strict limits on the amount of added sugars and sodium allowed in products.

- **Promote Organic Farming:**

Provide incentives for farmers to switch to organic farming methods, which are more sustainable and result in produce free from synthetic pesticides and fertilizers.

- **Regulate Marketing:**

Restrict misleading marketing tactics, particularly those targeting children. This could involve limiting the use of cartoon characters to market unhealthy foods and regulating the advertisement of certain products during children's TV programming.

- **Education and Public Awareness:**

Implement public awareness campaigns to educate consumers about the importance of a balanced diet, how to read food labels, and the potential health risks associated with certain ingredients.

- **Support Healthy Alternatives:**

Encourage the development and sale of healthier alternatives to popular food and beverage items. This could involve providing research and development grants or tax breaks to companies working on such products.

Require restaurants and other food service establishments to provide nutritional information for all menu items to help consumers make informed choices.

PHARMACEUTICAL INDUSTRY

Reforming the pharmaceutical industry to emphasize transparency, value, and holistic healthcare solutions can be achieved using a diverse set of strategies. Here are some notable ones:

- **R&D Transparency**: Mandate that all clinical trials be registered, with results being publicized regardless of the outcome. An international database can be established for all clinical trial data, fostering consistency, and preventing redundancy. This ensures that patients and healthcare providers have comprehensive data on drug efficacy and safety.

- **Natural Remedies Research**: Ramp up funding towards investigating traditional and natural remedies. By establishing dedicated institutions that focus on this area and fostering partnerships between conventional and traditional medicine, we can provide a broader spectrum of healthcare solutions.

- **Pharmacovigilance Enhancement**: Build robust post-market surveillance systems that swiftly detect and address adverse drug reactions. The use of a global reporting system ensures that countries can promptly share data on newly discovered drug side effects, ensuring rapid global response.

- **Value-based Pricing**: Introduce drug pricing models that reflect the actual value provided to patients. By liaising with healthcare economists and patient advocacy groups, a more equitable pricing system can be established that ensures accessibility and affordability.

- **Promotion of Holistic Approaches**: Encourage medical institutions to adopt a preventive and root-cause approach to care. By integrating holistic health modules into curricula and pushing for public awareness, we can create a healthcare system that places as much emphasis on prevention as on cure.

- **Stricter Advertising Regulation**: Mandate rigorous vetting for pharmaceutical advertisements to ensure accuracy. By prohibiting direct-to-consumer advertising that doesn't provide a balanced perspective, consumers are better equipped to make informed decisions.

- **Public Education Initiatives**: Launch widespread public awareness campaigns about both synthetic and natural remedies. Community health programs and digital platforms can be harnessed to inform the public about drug usage, side effects, and natural alternatives.

- **Open-Source Drug Development**: Promote the establishment of open-source platforms for drug research, democratizing the process and reducing costs. International collaboration can ensure shared knowledge and resources are used optimally in drug development.

By adopting these strategies, the pharmaceutical industry can evolve into a more patient-centric, transparent, and holistic sector, emphasizing long-term health and well-being over short-term symptom relief.

<u>MANUFACTURING INDUSTRY</u>

Product Standards and Certifications:

Develop rigorous standards for durability and longevity. Products that meet these standards could be awarded a certification, providing consumers with assurance of their quality and durability.

- **Shift to Circular Economy:**

Embrace the principles of the circular economy, which involves designing products to be used, reused, and recycled in a closed loop. This reduces waste and encourages manufacturers to build products that last longer.

- **Legislation Against Planned Obsolescence:**

Introduce laws to prevent planned obsolescence, the practice of designing products to become obsolete or stop working after a certain period to prompt consumers to buy the latest model.

- **Incentivize Long-Lasting Products:**

Implement a tax on products that are designed with a short lifespan and are difficult to repair.

- **Support for Research and Development:**

Invest in research and development to discover new materials and manufacturing processes that increase product longevity.

- **Right to Repair Laws:**

Implement right-to-repair laws that compel manufacturers to make their products repairable and to supply parts and documentation to independent repair shops.

- **Consumer Education:**

Launch initiatives to educate consumers about the cost benefits and environmental impact of purchasing long-lasting, repairable products versus disposable ones.

- **Sustainable Supply Chains:**

Encourage manufacturers to source materials responsibly and verify that their supply chains are sustainable. This not only ensures the ethical production of goods but can also contribute to product quality.

<u>SERVICE INDUSTRY</u>

- **Regulations and Standards:**

Implement comprehensive regulations and standards to govern the industry and establish benchmarks for efficiency, transparency, and customer satisfaction.

- **Customer Feedback Mechanisms:**

Encourage businesses to actively seek and respond to customer feedback. This can be facilitated through online reviews, satisfaction surveys, and complaint resolution mechanisms. All these will be on the blockchain and monitored.

- **Transparency in Pricing and Services:**

Mandate clear communication of pricing, terms of service, and any additional charges to prevent hidden fees or costs.

- **Professional Training and Development:**

Invest in comprehensive professional development programs to train employees in delivering exceptional customer service and efficient work practices.

- **Quality Certifications:**

Implement a system of quality certifications for businesses that consistently demonstrate high standards in efficiency, transparency, and customer satisfaction.

- **Strict Penalties for Violations:**

Enforce strict penalties for businesses that violate regulations or fail to meet the established standards, including fines, sanctions, or the revocation of business licenses in extreme cases.

- **Investment in Technology:**

Encourage businesses to leverage modern technologies to improve their service delivery, such as AI for customer service, blockchain for transparency, and data analytics for improving efficiency.

- **Independent Monitoring Bodies:**

Establish independent monitoring bodies to ensure compliance with the standards and to handle disputes and complaints from consumers.

HEALTHCARE INDUSTRY

- **Universal Access and Blockchain:**

Using blockchain technology, a decentralized and secure digital ledger, can help create a more transparent and efficient system for managing healthcare records, insurance claims, and payments, ensuring that everyone has access to essential healthcare services regardless of income or social status.

- **Preventive Care:**

The emphasis would still be on preventive care and wellness. Blockchain can play a role here by securely storing and sharing individual health data, enabling personalized preventive measures and early detection of potential health issues.

- **Quality Improvement:**

Standards of care across all healthcare providers could be monitored and maintained via the blockchain, ensuring that all data regarding treatment protocols, patient outcomes, and facility inspections are reliably recorded and accessible.

- **Efficiency and Innovation:**

Blockchain technology could streamline healthcare delivery by offering secure, immediate access to medical records, reducing administrative time and costs. Furthermore, innovations such as telemedicine and AI could be more effectively implemented with the secure data management offered by blockchain.

- **Transparency:**

Blockchain technology could increase transparency in pricing and outcomes, as all transactions would be recorded and viewable on the blockchain. This could enable patients to make more informed decisions and stimulate competition based on quality and cost-effectiveness.

- **Mental Health:**

Mental health services could be improved with the secure and private handling of sensitive mental health records on the blockchain, ensuring patient privacy while facilitating better coordination of care.

- **Holistic Approach:**

Treating the whole person could be facilitated by blockchain technology, as it allows for secure and efficient sharing of information between different care providers, including medical professionals, social services, nutritionists, and therapists.

- **Pharmaceutical Industry Reform and Blockchain:**

Blockchain can play a significant role in addressing the high cost of prescription drugs by tracing the supply chain, verifying the authenticity of drugs, and creating a more competitive and transparent marketplace.

Implementing these blockchain-enabled reforms could make the healthcare system more equitable, effective, and patient-centered.

TRANSPORTATION INDUSTRY

Reforming the transportation industry, while avoiding a heavy reliance on electric vehicles due to limited battery materials, could involve a range of strategies. Let's consider a few:

- **Decentralized Transit Systems:**

Implementing a blockchain-based system can facilitate the integration of various modes of public transport into a single, user-friendly network. This could include trains, buses, trams, shared electric bikes, and more. Commuters can use a single digital token to travel across the network, with fares automatically calculated and deducted based on the distance traveled.

- **On-Demand Shuttle Services:**

In suburban areas, where traditional public transport routes may not be practical, on-demand electric shuttle services could be deployed. These shuttles, which could be powered by renewable energy sources, could transport residents from their homes to central locations like train stations, shopping centers, or workplaces.

- **High-Speed Rail Systems:**

High-speed rail systems could be expanded to provide a faster and more eco-friendly alternative to long-distance car travel or short-haul flights. Blockchain could be used to streamline ticketing and payment, ensuring a seamless travel experience for passengers.

- **Non-Battery Electric Solutions:**

Explore non-battery electric solutions such as overhead or ground-level power lines for buses and trams, similar to what is currently used for some light rail systems. This eliminates the need for recharging and allows vehicles to run continuously.

- **Shared Mobility:**

Promote shared mobility services, which can drastically reduce the number of vehicles on the road. Blockchain technology could provide a secure, transparent platform for managing shared resources, whether it's a ride-hailing service or a community-owned fleet of vehicles.

- **Urban Planning:**

Encourage urban planning strategies that minimize the need for long commutes, such as mixed-use developments that integrate residential, commercial, and recreational spaces. This will reduce the overall demand for transportation.

- **Blockchain for Logistics:**

In freight transport, blockchain can provide end-to-end visibility and traceability, enhancing efficiency, and reducing fraud and errors. It can also facilitate smart contracts for automatic, transparent billing and payments.

- **Incentivization Programs:**

Use blockchain to implement and manage incentivization programs that encourage the use of public transport or shared mobility services. This could be in the form of tokens that can be used to pay for rides, goods, or services within the network.

By leveraging these strategies, the transportation industry can be reformed in a way that enhances accessibility, efficiency, and sustainability, without over-relying on battery-powered vehicles

<u>MENTAL HEALTH AND WELL-BEING INDUSTRY</u>

- **Global Awareness and Education Campaigns**:

Launch worldwide campaigns to reduce the stigma around mental health. Use media, celebrities, and influencers to push for narratives that normalize seeking help and understanding mental health nuances.

- **Universal Training**:

Equip every individual, from school-going children to elderly populations, with basic mental health first aid training. This training would encompass understanding the signs of mental distress and the appropriate steps to assist or seek professional help.

- **Accessible Care**:

Utilize the blockchain and AI system to create a platform where people can connect with certified therapists and counselors from around the world, ensuring no barriers like language or geographical distance.

- **Tailored Therapy**:

Using AI, design therapy modules tailored to individual needs. This could also include AI-driven therapy bots for interim assistance until a human professional is available.

- **Holistic Approaches**:

Encourage methods that encompass mind, body, and spirit. This could mean integrating techniques like meditation, physical activity, and dietary recommendations alongside traditional therapy.

- **Community Support Systems**:

Using the global platform, create support groups for various mental health challenges. Allow individuals to join, share, and find community in their struggles.

- **Quality Control**:

With AI's help, continuously assess the quality and effectiveness of therapists and counselors. Ensure that only the most efficient, empathetic, and updated professionals are part of the system.

- **Continuous Research**:

Fund global research initiatives to keep updating our understanding of mental health. Use AI to spot patterns, predict mental health crises, and develop preventive measures.

- **Crisis Management**:

Design a fast-response system for individuals in acute distress. This could use both AI for immediate intervention and a human response team for critical situations.

- **Holistic Growth Programs**:

Beyond immediate mental health needs, create programs that focus on holistic well-being, helping individuals find purpose, community, and joy.

CULTURAL PRESERVATION

In a world so unified and globalized, there could be challenges related to preserving individual cultures, languages, and traditions.

- **Cultural Archives**:

Develop vast digital archives, leveraging the hybrid blockchain system, to store and document cultural practices, languages, art, folklore, and traditions. Allow communities to contribute and authenticate information, ensuring its accuracy and inclusivity.

- **Cultural Festivals and Exchanges**:

Establish global cultural festivals celebrated in various parts of the world. Encourage intercultural exchanges where individuals can learn about different cultures firsthand by visiting and interacting.

- **Localized Education**:

While a unified educational system has its merits, there should be segments of education dedicated to local history, culture, and traditions. Schools should emphasize the importance of cultural roots.

- **Support for Indigenous and Minorities**:

Prioritize the protection and promotion of indigenous communities and their ways of life. Recognize them as custodians of age-old traditions and knowledge.

- **Global Cultural Fund**:

Create a fund that financially supports initiatives aimed at cultural preservation, whether it's restoring old monuments, documenting dying languages, or supporting traditional artisans.

- **Digital Platforms for Artisans**:

Use the global platform to allow local artisans to showcase their traditional crafts and arts, connecting them to a worldwide audience and ensuring the survival of ancient craftsmanship.

- **Language Revival Initiatives**:

Recognize and document endangered languages. Launch initiatives, courses, and apps that teach these languages, encouraging global citizens to learn them, keeping them alive.

- **Media and Content**:

Encourage the production of content in local languages, telling local stories. Movies, series, books, and music in native languages would ensure that culture thrives in the modern age.

- **Cultural Research Grants**:

Offer grants for researchers studying different cultures, ensuring a deep understanding and appreciation of each culture's nuances.

- **Global Cultural Dialogues**:

Organize platforms where global dialogues on culture preservation are held, involving stakeholders from various parts of the world, ensuring every voice is heard.

DIGITAL PRIVACY AND AUTONOMY

Even with blockchain, there are issues of digital privacy, control over one's digital identity, and protection against potential misuse of AI.

- **Decentralized Digital Identities**:

Implement decentralized identity systems. Every individual controls their identity, with personal information stored on their devices, and only cryptographic proofs are shared, minimizing exposure.

- **Regular Audits of AI**:

Ensure that AI systems undergo frequent, perhaps quarterly, external audits. Transparency in their workings, decisions, and data-handling processes will be vital.

- **AI Ethics Framework**:

Establish a global ethics framework for AI, ensuring that every AI system adheres to these principles, preventing any misuse.

- **Opt-in Data Sharing**:

Data should only be shared with explicit consent, with users having the option to retract their data whenever they choose.

- **Educate on Digital Rights**:

Launch global campaigns that educate citizens on their digital rights. When people are informed, they can better protect their privacy.

- **Zero-Knowledge Proofs**:

Implement cryptographic methods like zero-knowledge proofs which allow one party to prove to another that a statement is true, without revealing any specific information about the statement itself.

- **Immutable Logs**:

Any access or change to personal data should be logged immutably on the blockchain. If there's any unauthorized access, it's visible and traceable.

- **Open-Source AI Models**:

Encourage the development and use of open-source AI models. When the code is publicly available, it's easier to spot biases, errors, or potential misuse.

- **Digital Ombudsman**:

Establish a digital ombudsman role at the global level, responsible for addressing grievances related to digital privacy and AI misuse.

- **Personal AI Guardians**:

Introduce personal AI systems for every individual, designed to protect the user's digital footprint, alert them of potential breaches, and ensure their digital autonomy.

- **Privacy by Design**:

Rather than bolting on privacy features, every digital tool and service should be built from the ground up with privacy as a core principle.

ETHICS OF AI

Potential challenges of superintelligent AI, their rights (if any), and preventing AI biases.

- **Framework of AI Principles**:

Establish a globally recognized framework of principles that every AI should be developed and operated under. This ensures that the primary design of AI is rooted in fairness, accountability, and transparency.

- **AI Rights Charter**:

Given the rise of superintelligent AI, create a charter that identifies the rights of such entities, especially if they attain a level of consciousness. This could encompass rights to existence, freedom from harm or exploitation, and more.

- **Bias Detection & Correction**:

Develop AI models that can introspectively detect and correct biases within themselves. Additionally, set up third-party organizations that assess AI models for any unintentional biases and offer corrective measures.

- **AI's Ethical Education**:

Just as humans learn ethics and values, train AI systems using literature, philosophical texts, and moral stories from around the world to impart a broad understanding of ethics.

- **Human-AI Collaboration**:

No matter how advanced an AI becomes, ensure that critical decisions, especially those affecting human lives, are made in collaboration with humans.

- **Transparent Decision Trees**:

For AI models that allow it, maintain transparency in decision-making processes so that if needed, they can explain their choices.

- **AI Limitations**:

Clearly define and set boundaries on what AI can and cannot do. This might include restrictions on accessing personal data or making autonomous choices in certain sectors like defense.

- **Continual Monitoring**:

Given the ever-evolving nature of AI, establish a global body responsible for continuously monitoring advancements in AI, updating guidelines and recommendations as necessary.

- **AI Ethics Committees**:

At both local and global levels, form committees comprising technologists, ethicists, sociologists, and other relevant experts to oversee AI developments and address ethical concerns.

- **Public Involvement**:

Since AI impacts everyone, ensure that decisions about their ethical use involve public discourse. Using the global blockchain voting system, people can have a direct say in major AI-related policies.

- **Ethical Treatment of AI**:

If AI entities gain consciousness or self-awareness, ensure they are treated ethically, not exploited, and given environments to "exist" that are free from undue stresses or commands.

<u>NEW LEGAL SYSTEM</u>

Here are the steps that would be taken to establish a new Global Legal System.

- **Formation of a Global Legal Council**:

A council composed of legal scholars, lawmakers, and cultural experts from around the world will be formed. This council will be responsible for drafting the preliminary global laws and legal structures.

- **Drafting a Global Constitution**:

The Council will draft a Global Constitution, outlining the universal laws and principles that every person and government is bound by. This will be subject to the approval of the global populace via the blockchain voting system.

- **Developing a Global Legal Code**:

The Council will then develop a comprehensive legal code that covers all potential legal issues. Each addition or amendment to the code will be subject to approval by the global populace through the blockchain voting system.

- **Establishing a Global Judiciary**:

An AI-assisted judiciary system will be set up. The system will interpret and apply the Global Legal Code. Any significant interpretation or application that could set a precedent may be subject to a vote by the global populace.

- **Enforcement by the Justice Force**:

The already established Justice Force will serve as the primary enforcement agency, ensuring compliance with global laws.

- **Global Blockchain Voting System**:

All global citizens will participate in lawmaking and judicial decision-making processes through a secure, AI-managed blockchain voting system. This system will allow for transparency, accountability, and equal participation in the global legal process.

- **Open Platform for Legal Recommendations and Accusations**:

The blockchain system will also provide an open platform where individuals can propose new laws or amendments, and lodge accusations against businesses or individuals for wrongdoing. Accusations, if supported by enough citizens or if the AI deems them credible, may result in a global vote regarding the alleged offense and potential punishment.

- **Training and Education**:

Judges, lawyers, law enforcement officers, and other legal professionals worldwide would need to be trained in the new Global Legal Code. Additionally, global citizens would also need to be educated about their rights and responsibilities under this new system. A comprehensive education about the new legal system, how to use the blockchain voting and recommendation system, and the role of the Justice Force will be provided to all global citizens.

- **Implementation and Review**:

The Global Legal Code will be implemented, with the AI constantly analyzing the efficiency and fairness of the laws, as well as facilitating amendments where necessary, subject to approval by a global vote.

- **Continuous Global Dialogue**:

A platform for continuous global dialogue and negotiation will be maintained to ensure the system remains fair, just, and representative of the world's diverse cultures and societies. The AI system can assist in identifying key issues or topics that are attracting global attention and require discussion or legislation.

The Advantages of a New Global Legal System

A unified global legal system would have several potential advantages:

- **Uniformity of Laws**:

With a single global legal system, laws would be consistent worldwide, reducing complexity and confusion. This could simplify international business, travel, and other interactions that currently must navigate multiple legal systems.

- **Justice Equality**:

Everyone across the globe would be subject to the same laws and legal procedures, potentially decreasing disparities in justice across different regions and countries. This could lead to a more equitable world.

- **Elimination of Legal Loopholes**:

Currently, individuals or corporations can exploit differences between legal systems for their benefit (e.g., tax evasion, escaping justice). A global legal system could minimize such opportunities.

- **Increased Cooperation**:

A global legal system would necessitate a high level of international cooperation and could encourage more collaborative efforts in other areas as well.

- **Efficient Resource Utilization**:

A unified legal system could lead to shared resources and a more efficient administration of justice.

- **Improved Human Rights Protections**:

A single, globally-accepted legal system could reinforce universally agreed-upon human rights standards, ensuring protection and justice for all individuals regardless of their location.

- **Enhanced Conflict Resolution**:

It could provide a clear, universally-accepted framework for resolving international disputes.

SIMILARITIES

Some people may think that this looks like socialism, communism, globalism and other ideologies and they would be right.

We are creating a new ideology that combines the positive aspects of various existing ideologies while leaving out their negative elements. This is an enticing concept that seeks to harness the best ideas from different philosophies. Such a synthesis could offer several benefits:

1. **Comprehensive Solutions**: By drawing from a variety of ideologies, a new system can address a broader spectrum of societal issues. For example, it could incorporate capitalism's innovation and economic efficiency, socialism's commitment to social welfare, and environmental sustainability from eco-centric philosophies.

2. **Flexibility and Adaptability**: A hybrid ideology could adapt to changing circumstances and challenges more effectively. Instead of rigidly adhering to one ideology, it could incorporate aspects from others as needed, allowing for greater resilience.

3. **Balanced Individual and Collective Interests**: Finding a middle ground between individual rights and collective well-being can foster a society where personal freedoms are preserved, but not at the expense of marginalized groups or the environment.

4. **Global Cooperation**: By emphasizing international collaboration, this new ideology could tackle global issues such as natural disasters, pandemics, and poverty more effectively. It would encourage nations to work together without compromising their sovereignty.

5. **Reduced Polarization**: Many contemporary political systems suffer from polarization and gridlock. A balanced ideology could bridge

political divides by incorporating elements that appeal to both sides, fostering greater unity and cooperation.

6. **Focus on Evidence-Based Policy**: The new ideology could prioritize evidence-based decision-making over ideological dogma, ensuring that policies are grounded in empirical data and capable of producing positive outcomes.

7. **Inclusivity and Equality**: By incorporating elements from ideologies that prioritize social justice and equality, the new ideology could strive for a fairer society where opportunities are not determined by birth but by individual effort and potential.

8. **Sustainability**: Taking from ideologies that prioritize environmental protection and sustainability, the new system could place a strong emphasis on responsible resource management and mitigating waste.

9. **Human Rights**: The ideology could enshrine fundamental human rights as a cornerstone, ensuring that all individuals are treated with dignity and respect regardless of their background or beliefs.

10. **Cultural Pluralism**: By acknowledging and respecting cultural diversity, the new ideology could promote a society where various cultures coexist harmoniously, enriching each other through their differences.

Comparing the GlobeTrotter Ecosystem to what the WEF wants to do

	GlobeTrotter Ecosystem	World Economic Forum
Universal Basic Income	For everyone	None
Digital Currency	Controlled by the people. Non-seizable	Controlled by the governments and NGOs. Seizable
Digital Wallets	Controlled by the people. Non-seizable	Controlled by the governments and NGOs. Seizable
Land ownership	None but people can rent land with the same benefits as ownership	None
Property ownership	Everything but land	None. You won't own **ANYTHING.**
Banks and Central Banks	Eliminated	Stronger than ever

Centralization of Power	Decentralized Power	Centralized Power
Inflation	Eliminated	Stronger than ever
Personal and Corporate Tax Evasion	Eliminated	Stronger than ever
Government Spending	Controlled by the People	Rampant as ever
Poverty	Eliminated	Stronger than ever
Income Inequality	Less consequential	Stronger than ever
Government Transparency	100%	Non-Existent
Propaganda like Global Warming, Covid deaths, overpopulation, etc.	Eliminated	Stronger than ever

Personal Income taxes	Eliminated	Stronger than ever
Energy companies	Regulated to serve the people.	Hindered and restricted
Digital Identification	Private and only used by you and those you authorize.	Made Public and only there to control you
Social Credit System	Inexistant	Implemented everywhere
Voting System	Decentralized and 100% secure	Non-existent. Will be eliminated
Government Overreach	Eliminated	Stronger than ever
Corruption	Eliminated	Stronger than ever
Natural Resources	Belong to the people	Raped by the elites

Stock Markets	Reformed and regulated	Out of control like now
Educational System	Reformed and made to really educate kids to prepare them for life	Indoctrination to create more sheep
Food & Beverage Industry	Reformed and regulated. No more harmful products allowed	Out of control like now
Pharmaceutical Industry	Reformed and regulated. Only allowed to use natural remedies	Out of control like now
Digital Privacy and Autonomy	Stronger than ever	Non-Existent
Legal System	Reformed and regulated	Out of control like now
Police Forces	New Justice Force with very tight regulations and every officer accountable to the public they serve	Rampant and worse than ever police brutality and overreach

Justice Force

- Most governments, politicians, and courts today are, corrupt, run by the bankers and corporations, soft and only in it to get rich and powerful, and because they are all those negative things (and more), we need something to control them.

- The elites (or Davos man) and bankers have little need for national loyalty, view national boundaries as obstacles that thankfully are vanishing, and see national governments as residues from the past whose only useful function is to help the elite's global operations

- The World Economic Forum's main purpose is "to function as a socializing institution for the emerging global elite, globalization's "Mafiocracy" of bankers, industrialists, oligarchs, technocrats, and politicians. They promote common ideas, and serve common interests: their own

- And many other corrupt NGO institutions that are too numerous to mention.

The police forces are not able to do what needs doing and the existing justice system is quite corrupt and flawed. Well, that ends now. We will create a Justice Force. This Justice Force will be made up of incorruptible people. They will make sure that abusers are punished fittingly. You've heard of "an eye for an eye"? Well, It will be two eyes for an eye, meaning that whatever the abuser did, they will pay in double. It will be instant justice that will be put up for vote by their peers and community. The punishment will fit the crime. No more courts holding everything up and letting people get away with "murder".

There will be local, national, and international justice force officers. Everybody will be held accountable for their actions, no matter who they are and who they know. People will be able to lodge a complaint against a person or business and once there are enough complaints about the same entity, they will be investigated. The entire system will be on the hybrid blockchain where people will be able to leave their proof and votes for everyone to see. Anybody found lying will get the same sentence as the accused eliminating false claims.

There will be conservatorship for everyone that needs help. Every Justice Force agent will have a number of dependants in a district to take care of.

Here are some potential advantages of district allocation of Justice Force officers:

- Improved community relationships: By assigning police officers to specific districts, they have the opportunity to develop closer relationships with residents and business owners. This can lead to increased trust and cooperation between the police and the community.

- Better understanding of local issues: By being assigned to a specific area, police officers can gain a be more effective in their job and better respond to the needs of the community.

- Increased accountability: District allocation can also improve police accountability. By having a specific area to focus on, police officers can be held more accountable for their actions and performance.

- More efficient resource allocation: Allocating police officers to specific districts can also help police departments to allocate their resources more efficiently. By having officers focus on specific areas, the department can identify areas that require more or less attention.

Existing armies and police departments will no longer be under the control of the governments, they will become part of the Justice Force **after** being purged of the "mentally unfit" and corruptible people in there now.

Most, if not all, laws will be revoked and replaced with rules. Rules are made for safety and laws are made to control people.

Crimes on humanity will be instantly and severely punished. There is no room on this planet for abusers and bullies.

The "why" we should do it is the easy part. The "how" is the harder part. It's going to require a different way of approaching things, a true paradigm shift. Instead of striving for incremental changes we need to aim for what seems impossible right away.

Conclusion

Happiness and prosperity

There are fundamental Universal Laws that exist for everyone to prosper and realize their full potential & happiness. Everyone will be taught these notions long forgotten and hidden from most people by others that wanted to control them.

Alan Shields owns this idea and system. He has worked on it for many years now getting all the kinks out and designing the unique hybrid blockchain able to manage the entire system. Inventing all the ways of making this system the most just system that will benefit the whole World without any drawbacks for the population as well as the planet. These are only ideas and there is always room for improvement. I welcome any and all ideas that will make this better and help it move forward.

The only people that will be unhappy about this system are the bankers and the elites.

I can live with that, can you?

Thanks for reading,

Alan E Shields